ALSACE

A WINE LOVER'S TOURING GUIDE

If no address is given for a hotel, park, wine cellar or other place of interest, the reader may assume that everyone in the locality will be able to give directions or that signs point the way out.

Hubrecht Duijker

Alsace

A wine lover's touring guide

Het Spectrum

Books by Het Spectrum are brought onto the market by:
Publishing House Het Spectrum Ltd.
Postbus 2073
3500 GB Utrecht
The Netherlands

Copyright © 1993 by Hubrecht Duijker
Cover design: Alpha Design, Leusden, The Netherlands
Photos: Hubrecht Duijker
Translation: Paul Goodman
Lay out/Typesetting: G.A.C.W. Willemsen
Lithography:RCA, Zwolle, The Netherlands
Cartography: TOP 250 n° 104 © IGN Paris 1992 - Autorisation n° 30.3031
Printing: Aubin Imprimeur, Ligué, France
First edition: 1993
Cover photo: The attractive village of Turckheim

The author will be grateful for any suggestions, ideas and comments concerning
this guide. You may send them to the above address, attn. Hubrecht Duijker.

ISBN 1 85365 301 2

British Library Cataloguing-in-Publication Data.
A catalogue record for this book is available from the British Library.

CONTENTS

INTRODUCTION

Alsace lies in the outermost northeastern part of France, between the Rhine and the Vosges mountains. This range has a few peaks that rise to over 1300 or even 1400 metres and stretches in length to approximately 170 kilometres. Although the massif still boasts many mountains of granite, for centuries it has also provided the pink sandstone with which numerous houses and churches have been built.

The Vosges not only forms a watershed between the basins of the Rhine and the Moselle – which flow into each other much further to the north – it also protects Alsace from the humid western winds. For this reason the area enjoys a dry climate, despite its northern location. It is estimated that after Perpignan, Colmar is probably the driest city in France. On average a mere 480 millimetres of rain fall there each year, in contrast to over 2000 in the Vosges. In this climate many varieties of vegetables and fruit flourish, as well as Mediterranean plants. Parts of Alsace are truly a botanical paradise: near the village of

Twilight in the wine village of Ammerschwihr.

Westhalten, on the hill of Zinnkoepflé, one may find no less than 550 varieties that are native to the South of France. Grapes also grow to perfection here – as they have done for centuries. In 58 BC Alsace was conquered by Julius Caesar, after which the Romans occupied it for a few hundred years. From excavations made in wine villages such as Wettolsheim and Eguisheim, it appears that the Romans made wine. Since time immemorial, the best vineyards of Alsace have been on the foothills on the eastern side of the Vosges. Here the grapevines can benefit most from the warm sun and the shelter of the nearby mountains. The soil of Alsace shows a large variation in types, almost all of which are suitable for viniculture.

Two Departments

From an administrative point of view Alsace consists of two departments: Bas-Rhin in the north and Haut-Rhin in the south. The demarcation line lies between Strasbourg and Colmar, running near the town of Sélestat and the castle of Haut-Koenigsbourg, which, from its vantage point on a high mountain crest, dominates the expansive landscape. A considerable part of Alsace consists of the fertile, flat and fairly boring Rhine plain, while another area is extremely mountainous, with forests, meadows and bare rock. The wine area – the subject of this guide – is situated in a narrow strip between these zones. Its beauty is not easily surpassed in France – or elsewhere – while it also possesses a very individual character.

Fairy Tale Villages

Through its landscape alone, the wine area is sure to charm the visitor. Everywhere one sees green hills, of all possible shapes and sizes, sometimes low and round, in other places high and steep – with all variations in between. To the east the horizon is formed by the shadowy contours of the Black Forest on the far bank of the Rhine, while, on the western side, the Vosges consistently offer a spectacular backdrop. The dark green of the coniferous and deciduous trees on the mountains stands out against the lighter tints of the grapevines, a contrast that is increased in late autumn as the vineyards develop a brillant

Hunawihr, with the castles of Ribeauvillé in the background.

mixture of all possible shades of gold, yellow and brown, which glow with light in the baking autumn sun.

However, Alsace has even more to offer the visitor: it has all the qualities of a prosperous wine area. Most villages appear to have been plucked from a fairy tale by the brothers Grimm or from an old picture book. They form a romantic scene of half-timbered houses, churches, city halls in Renaissance style, fortified portals and towers, old wells and fountains. In spring and summer, flowers abound. House façades, galleries and balconies seem weighed down with their abundance of brilliant flowers, with geraniums especially popular everywhere; people often fill the fountain basins with them. The streets are usually narrow, cobbled and not really suitable for traffic. The wine villages of Alsace lend themselves in particular to both short and longer walks; sauntering along, one is carried back in time to taste the atmosphere of Europe long ago. Elsewhere such villages would appear over-elaborate and pretentious, but in Alsace one senses the authenticity and sincerity with which such a unique inheritance is lovingly preserved. It is striking to note, for example, with how much care the walls have been painted in the proper colours and the façades decorated with suitable signboards.

Painted half-timbered house in Ottrott.

ROMANESQUE CHURCHES

In the villages and cities of Alsace there are many architectural styles to enjoy. Here and there, sarcophagi and other mortuary monuments from the Merovingian period are still to be found. Sometimes these are sited with apparent nonchalance, without a sign or any other marker. It is left to the visitor to discover them for himself. For example, in the village of Heiligenstein, a sarcophagus simply stands at the side of a fountain. Much more impressive are buildings in the Romanesque style. The churches can be recognized by their sober exterior, thick walls, small windows, carved tympana and the usually square clock towers. They generally date from the 11th and 12th centuries. A few examples are Saint-Pierre-et-Saint-Paul of Rosheim, Saint- Léger of

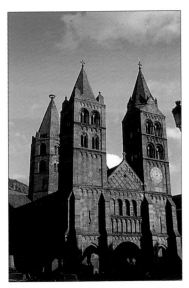

The Romanesque Saint-Léger in Guebwiller.

Guebwiller and the clock towers of Gueberschwihr.

GOTHIC AND RENAISSANCE

From the 13th to the 15th centuries, the Gothic style flourished in Alsace. This is also best represented by churches. Characteristic of the Gothic style is the vertical line, the pointed arch, at times almost lace-like carvings, the slender towering steeples and the many windows, including several rose windows. Just outside the wine area stands the famous Gothic cathedral of Strasbourg. Within the wine area are found, among others, the churches of Thann and Rouffach; the latter is also part Romanesque. In the 16th and the beginning of the 17th centuries, the Renaissance style appeared in Alsace. This can be seen in many stone houses, with stepped gables, bay windows, galleries and stylish ornaments. Many city administrators and wealthy patricians – among whom there were several wine-growers – built city halls and houses in this style. They are to be found everywhere in Alsace.

HALF-TIMBERED HOUSES

Most of the half-timbered houses were built in the 17th and 18th centuries. It is striking how much they vary: one cannot point to any type of unity. Contractors, architects and artisans apparently enjoyed giving every house its own look. They played especially with galleries, balconies, roofs, beam motifs and colours: not unusually made to order. In the course of the 17th century – after a badly battered Alsace became French – people also began to build in the Classical style. The buildings concerned are impressive in a very formal way, without much decoration or excess. A well-known example is the Notre-Dame church in Guebwiller, not far from the Romanesque Saint-Léger. In this village, in the same street, stand these two totally different churches, with, half way between, a Gothic town hall as well: this typifies Alsace.

Proud Traditions

On a human level, Alsace is also an attractive area. Few French regions have been hit so often by the ravages of war or known for so long the yoke of the conqueror yet, despite these troubles – or more precisely because of them – the Alsatians are optimistic lovers of life. This is made obvious not only by the presence of flowers everywhere, but also in the pleasure that they find at the table. Few French regions possess more good eating places, from simple *winstubs* to three-star restaurants. The Alsatians also have a sense of humour, even under difficult situations, as witnessed by the satirical cartoons of Hansi, who ridiculed the German occupiers. One well-known anecdote concerns the large statue of Christ that stands, with arms outspread, on the mountain top near Les Trois Epis. During the Second World War, the Germans wanted to destroy it because it was believed to have been paid for by rich Jews. An Alsatian is said to have asked them: 'Why do you want to do that? It's the only Alsatian to have received you with open arms.' The statue still stands in its lofty site.

In daily life and at school the Alsatian dialect is kept alive. Various publications even appear in dialect, including newspapers and books.

The active interest that the inhabitants maintain in their own region is shown by the many books that have been published solely about Alsace. Entirely appropriate to this outlook are the traditional

Façades decorated with flowers are also traditional.

costumes that young and old still wear on festive occasions. This does not mean that Alsatians are inward-looking, however, because their hospitality is proverbial. Anyone who visits the wine villages will experience this for themselves.

Historic Perspective

Due to its strategic position, on the border of present-day France and Germany, Alsace has often been involved in international conflicts. As wine dealer Jean Hugel once said: 'We are specialists in war and white wine.' In the distant past the Celts had to give way to the Romans, after Caesar had defeated Ariovistus in 58 BC. Half way through the 4th century, the Alemanni invaded and overran Alsace. Slowly, over the course of the 5th century, they were driven out by the Frankish dynasty of the Merovingians. The final, decisive battle took place in 496 near Wissembourg. The victor was Clovis, the first Christian king of the Franks. His followers established many settlements in Alsace and today many Alsatian villages bear names that are Frankish in origin. Moreover, in this region one can also find Frankish sarcophagi and various mortuary monuments.

The signboard of a wine house in Riquewihr.

Robber Knights

From the 7th century on, for a long the area was time ruled by dukes, among whom was the brutal Etichon, father of Odile who was later canonized (see the chapter concerning Obernai). In the 10th century Alsace came under German rule and was to remain so for 700 years. The power of the German emperors was, however, limited. The welfare or otherwise of the inhabitants was to a large degree determined by the dukes, counts and other *seigneurs*, who often behaved like robber knights. Silent witnesses to this period are the numerous castle ruins that brood like ghostly silhouettes on the mountain tops. As protection against attackers, villages and cities were frequently fortified. Moreover, districts formed alliances among themselves, with the purpose of protecting each other against enemies and also cooperating in other ways. The best known pact was the Décapole, a federation of ten Alsatian cities, established in the 14th century. These cities were Colmar, Haguenau, Kaysersberg, Mulhouse, Munster, Obernai, Rosheim, Sélestat, Turckheim and Wissembourg. Apart from secular rulers, Alsace has also known the power of the Church, such as the extremely powerful

In the Petite France suburb of Strasbourg, the Maison des Tanneurs (the house of the tanners), now a restaurant, stands by the Ill.

archbishop of Strasbourg. How strong the influence of the clergy was can be seen in the increase in the number of monasteries. In the 6th century Alsace had 40, in the 13th century 300. That the abbeys were also interested in secular affairs shows in the presence of tithe barns. In these *cours dimières* the mandatory contributions of the inhabitants were collected. Tiny Eguisheim alone contains six tithe barns.

War and Peace

In the 14th and 15th centuries the Alsace experienced a difficult time. The area was now ravaged by pestilence as well as war. In 1439 both the Armagnacs and the English invaded the region. Five years later Louis XI struck back and many villages were destroyed. The year 1525 was also a black year: approximately 20,000 peasants rose up against the rich clergy and aristocracy and were almost all killed by the duke of Lotharingen. From the second half of the 16th century until the beginning of the 17th century, the area knew a period of peace and prosperity and Alsace grew to be the richest and mostpopulated part of the Holy Roman Empire. Later than in neighbouring France, the influence of the Renaissance arrived, bringing more secular concepts of life and art. One sees this continually reflected in the numerous wonderful buildings that were constructed during this period.

THE THIRTY YEARS' WAR

This prosperity came to an abrupt end in 1618 with the outbreak of the Thirty Years' War. Alsace was the victim of various invasions. In particular, around 1633 the Swedes brought much destruction and cruelty. At the same time pestilence and starvation demanded a high toll. Peace returned in 1648. France received practically the whole of Alsace from the Habsburgs. King Louis xiv – who, when viewing the region, is supposed to have cried out: '*L'Alsace...quel beau jardin!*' – organized a repopulation plan. As the preference was for new inhabitants who were Catholic, many of them came from Switzerland. This explains why the Alsatian costume looks so much like that of Switzerland.

The attractive wine village of Turckheim.

THE MARSEILLAISE

In 1674 the German emperor made an attempt to win Alsace back when he invaded the region with 60,000 men. Near Turckheim in January of 1675, his army was defeated by a much smaller force under the leadership of Captain Turenne. Strasbourg, which had until then remained independent, was also joined to France in 1681. Over a century later, in 1792, the Marseillaise was sung for the first time. The French Revolution had begun and certain patriots were disturbed that they did not have an inspiring marching song. In one day Captain Claude Joseph Rouget de Lisle composed a song based on the expressions, cries and slogans that could be seen and heard over the whole city. In a tenor voice, he sang this 'War Song of the Rhine Army' on the evening of 26 April at the home of lord mayor Dietrich. The song was quickly adopted by volunteers from Marseille and thus received its present name. A modest plaque at number 4 place Broglie commemorates the event; a bank now occupies the spot.

Occupied Again and Again

In 1870 Napoleon III declared war on Germany, with the result was that Alsace was annexed to Germany. With this a sad period began. The Germans submitted the inhabitants to a regime that was so harsh that one in eight Alsatians fled the region. German was prescribed as the official language. In 1914 the First World War broke out. Particularly in the south of Alsace, there was heavy fighting, such as on the Vieil Armand mountain, where 30,000 French and Germans lost their lives. In 1918 the French flag was raised once more. A good two decades later,

Flowers and a bottle as a sign of welcome at the southern entry of Mittelwihr.

during the Second World War, the Germans reoccupied the area. This time around they practised a true reign of terror. Many young Alsatians were conscripted and sent to Russian front. Around 43,000 of these Malgré-nous perished and thousands of others landed up in Russian camps. The last of the survivors did not return until 1955. The final liberation, at the end of 1944, was overshadowed by heavy, destructive fighting in the 'Colmar Pocket', in which the villages of Ammerschwir, Bennwihr, Katzenthal, Mittelwihr and Sigolsheim were almost totally lost. Happily, it was possible to rebuild them in such a way that much of their original atmosphere and beauty was restored.

The only invaders Alsace knows nowadays are very peaceful tourists. In their own country, as well as among the other nations of Western Europe, the unique qualities of Alsace are enthusiastically valued by a growing number of people.

Viticulture and Wines

The vineyards of Alsace lie predominately along a strip, approximately 120 kilometres long, in the eastern foothills of the Vosges. The area begins at the height of Strasbourg and ends on the same level as Mulhouse, two cities built on the Rhine plain and which lie outside the wine region. Characteristic of Alsace – 13,000 hectares – is the small scale of winegrowing. Of approximately 7800 winegrowers, a good 80 per cent own less than 10 hectares and a good 45 per cent even less than five. A large group of the farmers therefore have too little land from which to work their own grapes into wine and afterwards bottle and sell it. As a result of this, wine production is, to an important degree, controlled by cooperatives and wine merchants. They collect the grapes or wines from small *viticulteurs* to make viable quantities. In this way about three-quarters of the total volume is brought to the market by *caves coopératives* and *négociants*. The remaining quarter is handled by private wine estates. Due to the fact that these are larger in number than the cooperatives and wine merchants, one mainly sees their names and signboards in the wine villages. Everywhere in Alsace wine may be bought directly from hundreds of farmers. For that matter, the cooperatives and wine merchants also sell quite a few bottles on the spot. In this way a small *négociant* in Riquewihr turns over no less than a tenth of his production.

The grapevines are sprayed to protect them from diseases.

NAMED AFTER GRAPES

Another characteristic of Alsace is that, in general, the wines are named after their grape variety. The winegrowers differentiate between noble and ordinary varieties. Gewurztraminer, Muscat, Pinot Noir, Riesling and Tokay Pinot Gris belong to the first category. The simpler varieties are Chasselas, Pinot Blanc and Sylvaner. Since 1970 the share of noble types has increased by more than half, with the result that they are now being cultivated on about 60 per cent of the wine ground. Apart from wines made from a select number of grape varieties, Alsace also produces blended wines. These are Edelzwicker – the simplest wine type – and Crément d'Alsace, a very successful sparkling wine. Moreover, all wines must be bottled in the region itself.

GRANDS CRUS

Wines from about fifty carefully selected vineyards may be produced with the title grand cru. The regulations relating to these wines are sig-

Display in Ammerschwihr.

nificantly stricter than those for the other qualities. For ordinary wines, with the name of origin Alsace, a maximum yield of 100 hectolitres per hectare holds. Grands cru vineyards, on the other hand, may not exceed a yield of 70 hectolitres per hectare. Moreover a higher minimum alcohol percentage prevails. Another limitation concerns the grape varieties allowed. All wines from Gewurztraminer, Muscat, Riesling and Tokay Pinot Gris grapes may be offered as grands crus. For a full list of the grands crus, see the appendix.

SPECIAL TITLES

Special titles can also appear on the labels of Alsatian wine. These always denote wine made from grapes that have been harvested late and contain much more sugar. Such wines are always more or less sweet and contain a relatively high alcohol percentage. For the title *vendange tardive*, enough sugar must be present in the juice of the muscat and riesling grapes for a potential alcohol percentage of 13 per cent, while this can run up to 15.1 per cent for *sélection des grains nobles*. The de-

mands are yet stricter for gewurztraminer and tokay pinot gris because here percentages of 14 and
16.4 per cent, respectively, hold.
Wines with the title *vendange tardive* generally taste slightly sweet,
while those with *sélection des
grains nobles* are pronouncedly
sweet. The prices of these types of
wine are extremely high. The
winegrowers see these titled wines
as their ultimate product and are
very proud of them. The question
is, however, whether these expensive, mild wines – which are being
made in increasing amounts – are
frightening off loyal and potential
users of the normal, reasonably
priced, dry wines?

Fountain in Obernai.

There now follows a short de-
scription of various types of wine made in Alsace.

CHASSELAS

While a generation ago chasselas represented one-fifth of the planting,
this is now down to a small percentage and even this share is falling.
Chasselas is practically never used on its own, but the producers who
do use it make a succulent, charming thirst-quencher. Generally, chasselas disappears anonymously into Edelzwicker.

CRÉMANT D'ALSACE

Thanks to the pioneering efforts of Dopff au Moulin, a wine merchant
in Riquewihr, sparkling Alsace wine is nowadays an important product. This carries the appellation of origin Crémant d'Alsace and is
made according to the Champagne method. Half a dozen grapes may
serve as a basis but in most cases the pinot blanc variety is used. There
also exist Crémants made solely from riesling and even chardonnay
grapes (the Burgundian sort, which, in Alsace, may only be made into
a sparkling wine). Besides white Crémant d'Alsace there is also rosé; by
definition, this contains part pinot noir.

EDELZWICKER

Edelzwicker is almost always a blended wine made exclusively from simple grape varieties: chasselas, pinot blanc, sylvaner. A sympathetic thirst-quencher at a friendly price is the result. This type of wine is frequently sold in litre bottles. Often the name Edelzwicker is on the label but many producers also use brand names. It may happen that an Edelzwicker rises above its lowly status; in that case noble grapes are also blended in.

Grape picking is still done by hand, as here in Katzenhal.

GEWURZTRAMINER

Once one has tasted a Gewurztraminer it is never forgotten for this is a very outstanding, spirited wine with a frequently sultry spiciness, together with an exotic fruit and a light muscat tone. The spiciness of the wine is also shown in the name, because '-Gewurz' is derived from the German word for spice. The classic table mate for a truly full Gewurztraminer – there are also lighter sorts – is Munster, a pithy, regional cheese. A white wine such as this may, without problem, be served after a dinner with red wines. About 20 per cent of the vineyards are planted with grapes of the same name.

MUSCAT

In the south of France the muscat grape gives heavy, sweet wines but in Alsace they are light and dry. The Muscats from this northern area smell and taste deliciously of freshly picked grapes. The Alsatians themselves consider their Muscat to be an ideal aperitif wine, although it tastes fine with, among other things, fish dishes with a mild sauce. Two variants of the Muscat grape grow in Alsace, the muscat à petits grains and the muscat ottonel. The latter was introduced because it is less prone to rotting and mould. Despite this, it remains difficult to bring in a good muscat harvest year in, year out. For this reason, its production represents only a small percentage of the total grapes.

PINOT BLANC

Just as with the muscat grape, two versions of the pinot blanc are planted: the ordinary pinot blanc and the auxer-
rois. Usually they are blended but there are
also producers who bottle them separately.
If a wine contains auxerrois, solely or in
part, it usually carries the names Auxerrois,
Klevner or Clevner. The average quality is
generally slightly higher than that of the
pure Pinot Blanc or the blended version.
Characteristic to all variants is a very sup-
ple, quite light taste and a soft freshness;
austere sourness is practically unkown. The
total share of pinot blanc is around 20 per
cent. A wine that should not be confused
with Klevner is Klevner de Heiligenstein.
This is a very rare wine type made from an
entirely different grape variety and it comes

In the village of Heiligenstein.

exclusively from the village of Heiligenstein (see page 40) and its nearby surroundings.

Sarcophagus before a fountain in Heiligenstein.

PINOT NOIR

The only blue variety of Alsace is
the pinot noir, of Burgundian origins. This variety is present on
about seven per cent of the wine
land. Formerly, the Alsatians exclusively made a dry rosé from it,
but nowadays more and more
true red wines are seen. A growing
number even undergo ripening in
small oak vats. In the soft taste there is often a fruity flavour, resem-
bling strawberries.

RIESLING

The riesling is a grape that ripens late and requires a lot of sun. Thanks
to the sheltered climate of Alsace, this variety is cultivated with great
success. It is also one of the stars of the area. Along with Gewurztraminer, Riesling has made Alsace more famous than any other wine. A
good Riesling is characterized by an elegant structure and a fresh taste

with breeding and refinement. Its aroma often reminds one of flowers as well as fruit, while there can also be a hint of spices present. Some Rieslings taste very charming in their earliest youth but others still contain a biting freshness and require a few years' patience. Riesling's share amounts to 20 per cent.

SYLVANER
Generally the sylvaner grape gives an easy, accessible white wine without a lot of depth or personality. There are exceptions to this, because, in vineyards rich in limestone, these varieties can give surprisingly delicious creations with a pithy, light taste of spice and fruit. Examples of this are the Sylvaners of the Zotzenberg vineyards in Mittelbergheim. Only 20 per cent of the vineyards contain this grape type.

TOKAY PINOT GRIS
Like the muscat grape, the pinot gris is a sensitive variety and, as a consequence, a very modest plant. Presumably the pinot gris came from Hungary centuries ago by the agency of General Schwendi (see Kientzheim), hence the prefix tokay. The wine made from this grape is one of the strongest of the region, with a full, sometimes almost

Rodern, where a great deal of pinot noir is grown.

thick, taste and a distinctive aroma of a light smoky taste combined with a touch of honey and a tinge of nut. In Alsace itself the Tokay Pinot Gris is considered to be the ideal wine for accompanying goose liver paté.

DISTILLATES
Wine is not the only beverage of Alsace. The area makes good beers and also bottles mineral water in a few of the villages (Ribeauvillé, Soultzmatt). Moreover, Alsace has a long tradition of distilling. Fruits, flowers, buds and roots from the nearby mountain forests, as well as from the fertile Rhine plain, have, for centuries, been made into *eaux - de vie*. There are some 30 different kinds of *eau-de-vie*. These can be bought everywhere and in Lapoutroie, not far from Kaysersberg, there is a museum devoted to them.

The Cuisine

Alsatians love to eat and drink. Bakers, butchers and market-vendors do good business in the area, hundreds of restaurants flourish and the local wines are avidly drunk. It's not for nothing that the Alsatian dialect has produced expressions such as 'On a full stomach sits a happy head' and 'Eating and drinking well keeps body and soul together'. The regional cuisine is rich in specialities. Without doubt, the most famous is *pâté de foie gras*. This was supposedly made for the first time by Jean-Pierre Clause in Strasbourg. The meltingly soft, luxurious-tasting goose liver (or duck liver) paté is made according to personal recipes by many restaurants. The classic wine to accompany this is Tokay Pinot Gris, although a Gewurztraminer or even a Riesling is no less suitable, above all when it comprises a firm, lightly sweet *vendange tardive* or *sélection des grains nobles*.

Tempting offer.

Nutritious and Savoury Delights

Tremendous amounts of sauerkraut are produced on the Rhine plain and another speciality is *choucroute à l'alsacienne*, which is eaten at home and in restaurants and makes a very nutritious dish. Apart from sauerkraut this consists of potatoes and often five or six different sorts of meat, among which one will find sausages, bacon and smoked shoulders of pork or calf. An excellent wine to drink with this is generally the Pinot Blanc. Also very filling and savoury is the traditional dish of *baeckeoffe* (also written variously as *baeckaoffa, beakoffa, bäckeofe, baekenoffa*). This is a stew of beef and lamb, with potatoes, vegetables and spices. Due to the length of preparation, many restaurants only serve it on particular days. All types of Pinot are suitable with it: Pinot Blanc, Pinot Noir, Tokay Pinot Gris.

Colmar's Saturday market.

FROM SNACKS TO SWEETS

Popular – above all on weekend evenings – is *tarte flambée* or *flamme-kueche*, a crispy, thin dough containing a creamy mixture of onion and bacon. Warm, savoury pies can also be found (such as *tarte à l'oignon*),

A cheese route runs through the Vosges.

as well as cold and warm meat patés (*en croûte* or not). Various dishes are prepared using Riesling, such as *coq au Riesling*. The same wine, but from a glass, tastes marvellous with *truite au bleu*. *Schiffala*, smoked shoulder of pork, is a regional dish that is often served with horseradish. Much hunting is done in the Vosges: in season there is a large choice of game in the restaurants. The meals can be brought to a close with a little Munster, a pithy, red cheese made on the farms in the Vosges. By tradition one sprinkles cummin over the cheese and drinks Gewurztraminer with it. Sweet desserts may be *kugelhopf* (or *kougelhopf*), a sort of sponge-cake, fruit pies or sorbet made from Marc de Gewurztraminer.

An inviting table at the Le Parc hotel in Obernai.

USING THIS GUIDE

In words and pictures, this guide follows the *route du vin* that runs through the entire Alsace. Only a small, isolated territory near Wis-

sembourg is not included. This is sited too far from the rest of the vineyards, at about 60 kilometers north of Strasbourg. The wine route is followed from north to south. One by one, each interesting village is described, complete with places of interest and other tourist tips. Where possible, hotels and restaurants are also recom-

Along the wine route.

mended, always with price indications. Moreover, the best wine producers have been mentioned for each community, along with notes about their best wines. This selection is one of the most complete ever made for Alsace. Information concerning annual wine festivals is likewise given. All the villages mentioned really do deserve to be visited; the best way to discover what they have to offer is to walk through them, even if it is only briefly.

HOTELS

When reserving a hotel room, always ask for peacefully situated rooms at the back or, ideally, around a possible inner courtyard. Watch out for the presence of loud and frequently rung church bells. When making the reservation, the latest time of arrival is usually given. If you think that you are going to arrive later, then call in order to

Hotel-restaurant in Gueberschwihr.

notify the proprietor. Mail or fax a written confirmation of a reservation. Apart from hotels, Alsace has privately rented rooms. These residences can be recognized by their signs, but a list of names and addresses is usually to be found at the city hall or *syndicat d'initiative*.

RESTAURANTS

Telephoning restaurants in advance is always recommended, either to make reservations or to make certain that they are open on a particular day. Experience has shown that it is wise to order *à la carte* menus, because it is cheaper. What's more the dishes will most likely be put together from market-fresh ingredients. A la carte, the best dishes are usually regional ones. Indeed it is also sensible

mainly to order wines from Alsace itself – if possible those from the village concerned. Such wines will be more carefully and expertly selected than wines from other French regions. A decanter of water may always be had free of price and mineral waters can, naturally, also be ordered.

Obernai can be viewed from a carriage.

WINEGROWERS

The Alsatian winegrowers are hospitable and will receive guests with pleasure – above all if they are sincerely interested in wine. It can therefore be of help to let them see this guide: someone who arrives by recommendation is usually greeted in a friendlier way than a passing stranger. When tasting the wines – and there may be many – it is normal to spit them out but ask first where you can do this! Never give the winegrower a tip, but buy at least one bottle as a token of thanks for the hospitality enjoyed. For those who do not speak French well, it is worth remembering that everyone in Alsace also speaks German. The use of English is also increasing.

Tapping the young wine in Marlenheim.

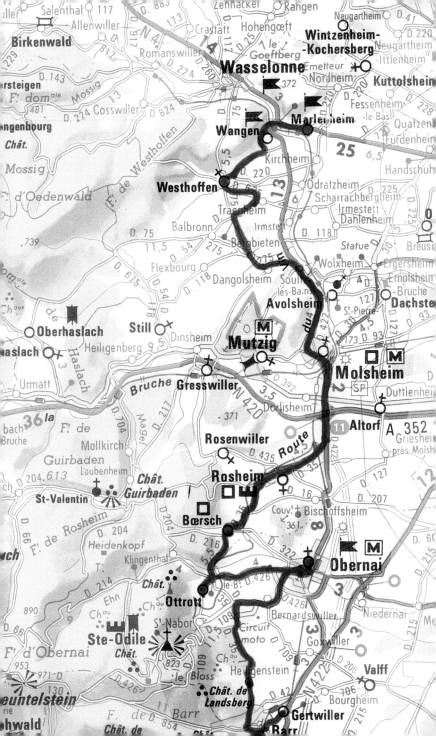

HOTEL
Hotellerie Reeb
℡ 88.87.52.70
Approximately 35 modernized rooms (up to circa FF 350). Reserve a room at the rear in order to avoid the busy traffic. In the comfortable, stylish restaurant there are generally four menus available (commencing at FF 100) and 10 wines available per glass. Taste, among others, the *preskopf au rosé de Marlenheim*.

RESTAURANTS
Le Cerf
℡ 88.87.73.73
This is one of the best places to dine in the entire Alsace. While retaining traditional values, the cooking is very inventive. This top address also asks top prices. The hotel rooms are fine, but not really peaceful due to the nearby main street.
Relais de la Route du Vin
℡ 88.87.77.86
A simple, cosy dining place with much wood. Regional dishes such as *choucroute* and *faisan à la vigneronne*. Friendly service.

MARLENHEIM

Marlenheim, which arose from the Roman settlement of Marilegium, is one of the oldest wine villages in Alsace. An historian mentions that in 589 the Merovingian monarch Childebert II condemned one of his unruly aristrocrats to work in the vineyards. At the time there was a magnificent Merovingian palace near Marlenheim.

The present municipality, housing almost 3000 inhabitants, lies along the busy *route nationale* 4, which connects Strasbourg with Paris. Traffic

Marlenheim is the start of the wine route.

roars straight through the winding main street. However, the old centre offers a peaceful and nostalgic atmosphere. Along slightly sloping streets stand half-timbered houses and the 18th century white church. At the end of the rue de la Chapelle there are steps forming part of the Stations of the Cross leading up to the Baroque

RECOMMENDED PRODUCERS
Serge Fend Especially recommended due to his wood-matured Pinot Noir.
Romain Fritsch Has land on the grand cru Steinklotz and produces, among others, a good Tokay Pinot Gris. Also makes Pinot Noir in red and rosé.
Laugel Metz Vins d'Alsace A large wine merchant which, at the beginning of the 1990s, was taken over by Rémy-Pannier, one of the most important wine firms of the Loire valley. In the assortment there are good Crémants and diverse successful, still wines, among them Riesling and Tokay Pinot Gris from the Steinklotz.

The sixth station of the cross on the way to Notre-Dame des Sept-Douleurs.

chapel of Notre-Dame des Sept-Douleurs. This stands in the middle of grapevines and offers a fine view of the entire village and its spacious surroundings. Southwards runs the *route du vin*, of which Marlenheim is the northernmost municipality. The Pinot Noir is the most famous wine of Marlenheim. The grape variety of the same name has been cultivated here for centuries. It is understood that in 1632 Swedish troops forgot their plundering after they had enjoyed plentiful amounts of Pinot Noir. The wine was (and is) also called 'Vorlauf', or 'first pressing'. The best local vineyard is the grand cru Steinklotz, which rises above the village.

TOURIST TIPS

- For walkers, Marlenheim has set out a *sentier viticole*. This route is clearly indicated and runs through the vineyards. The walk lasts approximately one and a half hours.
- On the 15th of August the village celebrates the folklore festival 'Le Mariage de l'Ami Fritz'.
- Marlenheim has a stork park – its location is indicated by signs.

Mosbach A quite extensive family wine estate, of which the cellars and the wine tavern lie on a small square along the main street. Certainly taste the Pinot Noir Vorlauf, the Tokay Pinot Gris and the Gewurztraminer.
Vinothèque du Lys A wine shop on the main street. It offers its own brand of

wines, Les Princes du Terroir.

RELATED TO WINE
- The harvest-home festival takes place during the second and third weekends of October.
- Taste the *vin nouveau* from pinot noir here at harvest time.

HOTEL
Diana
✆ 88.38.51.59
This modern hotel, dating from 1975, lies on the southern side of Molsheim, slightly outside the old centre. The angular, light green building has 60 rooms with elegant beds, a balcony (or entrance to the garden) and modern comforts. There is also a sauna and a shallow, finely designed swimming pool. The establishment has a '-gastronomic' restaurant (menus commencing at approximately FF 125) and a tavern. The prices for the rooms are around FF 350.

RESTAURANT
Au Cheval Blanc
✆ 88.38.16.87
Situated in an old building on the central square of Molsheim. The owner cooks *kugelhopf* from vegetables and duck in Muscat sauce. Attractively priced menu. It is also a hotel. Notice the wood carving along the façade.

IN AND AROUND MOLSHEIM

Between Marlenheim and Molsheim runs the *route du vin*, on which lie Wangen, with its medieval gateway towers, and Avolsheim, with its wine walk and Romanesque church. Slightly to

The chapel of Saint-Ulrich.

the south of Avolsheim a thousand-year-old tree stands near the chapel Dompeter. It is via this chapel that Christianity is said to have been brought to Alsace. The oldest part dates from the 11th century. Near the parish church of Avolsheim stands the small chapel of Saint-Ulrich. This was built around the year 1000. Molsheim is a good-sized city with about 7000 inhabitants. The centre is walled in part; one drives in on the southern side via the Tour de Forgerons, which is decorated with a gilded statue of the Virgin Mary. To the right of this is a large Jesuit monastery. The mostly cobbled streets lead to the triangular place de l'Hotel de Ville, where the Metzig stands. This marvellous Renaissance building was constructed in 1525 by the butchers' guild. In it is a small museum, with a *caveau* underneath.

RECOMMENDED PRODUCERS
MOLSHEIM
Antoine et Robert Klingenfus Located in a large building on the southern side of the city, they make not only Gewurztraminer Bruderthal and Muscat Finkenberg, but also a special Bugatti wine. This is called Pur Sang and is a Gewurztraminer.

Gérard Neumeyer Large winegrower, has a lot of land on the Bruderthal, resulting in an attractive Riesling, Tokay Pinot Gris and Gewurztraminer.
Bernard Weber A serious producer of, among others, a terrific Crémant, superior Sylvaner, Riesling Bruderthal and Tokay Pinot Gris Finkenberg.

The entrance of the Metzig, a Renaissance building in Molsheim.

Elsewhere in Molsheim there are other wonderful buildings. Not far behind the Metzig, the former Jesuit college, with its 17th century church full of religious art, and the former mint (16th century) can be found. Between the two world wars Ettore Bugatti made his famous cars in Molsheim. The city still has a Bugatti factory (aeroplane parts) and a Bugatti Foundation; most of the cars are in a museum in Mulhouse. The vineyards with the best reputation are the grand cru Bruderthal and the Finkenberg.

TOURIST TIPS
- For decades a regional wine exchange has taken place in Molsheim on the 1st of May.
- In Molsheim, on the second Sunday of October, the Grande Fête du Raisin is celebrated.

TRAENHEIM
La Cave du Roi Dagobert A small cooperative with a few good wines, such as Sylvaner, Tokay Pinot Gris and Gewurztraminer.
Philippe Lorentz His best Riesling is that of the grand cru Altenberg de Bergbieten.

Frédéric Mochel A small wine estate with excellent wines, such as the Gewurztraminer, Muscat and Riesling of the Altenberg de Bergbieten, Pinot Noir and Crémant. The family Mochel owns a winepress dating from 1669.

HOTEL
Hostellerie du Rosen-meer
℃ 88.50.43.29
A family who once ran an old *winstub*, built a modern hotel beside it in 1986. The reasonably large rooms are adequately furnished (with not enough light for reading). The prices run from FF 200 to about FF 500. No elevator. Hubert Maetz cooks inventively as shown in the dishes included in his most expensive menu, the *menu dégustation*.
The interior of the winstub is cosier than that of the dining room.

RESTAURANT
La Petite Auberge
℃ 88.50.40.60
Pleasant regional restaurant opposite the church of Saint-Etienne. Regional dishes such as *choucroute, baekeoffe* (usually on Saturdays), *côte de boeuf au Pinot Noir*. In season there are also oysters.

ROSHEIM

Those who follow the northern part of the Alsatian wine route must not miss out Rosheim, because, along the straight main street, one finds not only half-timbered houses and other lovely buildings but also the impressive church of Saint-Pierre et Saint-Paul. This large basilica, in the form of a cross, is one of the best preserved Romanesque monuments of Alsace. Work on it began in 1160 and it contains an organ by Silbermann from the year 1733. Further up the same street, past the massive Saint-Etienne church with

its four pillars, stands the oldest house in Alsace, the so-called Heidenhüss. This dates from the 12th century. From an eastern direction one drives into Rosheim via two gateways situated a few hundred metres from

A mural in the village centre.

RECOMMENDED PRODUCERS
Lucien Kirmann & Fils Their cellars are situated at the beginning of the street that runs straight through Rosheim, rue du Général de Gaulle, at number 2. The whole range, is available including Sylvaner and Riesling.
Remy Klein.Taste the Crémant here.

Jacques Maetz A small winegrower (the same family also runs the *Hostellerie du Rosenmeer*). Specialities are the soft, fresh Sylvaner Westerberg and the Pinot Blanc Auxerrois (two sorts from the Stufferein and Geiselmauer).

The austere Saint-Pierre et Saint-Paul is one of Alsace's best preserved Romanesque churches.

each other. A third gateway stands in the centre, along with a town hall and a fine well from 1605. Not far from this third gateway a baker has put up a colourful mural painting of a boy with wings. Rosheim has a long history. The village is first mentioned as Rodashaim in a document dating from 778. In 1212 mercenaries from Lotharingen attacked the village and began to plunder it. They drank so much wine that they were afterwards easily totally defeated by farmers led by a knight, Otto van Rodesheim. The event was given the name 'guerre des caves'. Nowadays wine lovers are hospitably received in the very same cellars.

TOURIST TIPS

- In the months of July and August the syndicat d'initiative organizes a free village walk twice in the week with commentary in French and German. On Tuesday evenings, in the same months, tourists can take part in an evening reception with wine tasting.
- A yearly floral procession takes place, usually on the first or second weekend after the 1st of September.

Façade decoration with winegrowing motif.

RESTAURANT
Le Châtelain
✆ 88.95.83.33
In the heart of Boersch a small speciality restaurant flourishes. The dining room is found on a *vide* (watch out for the low beam) and is tastefully furnished. There is also a tasting and reception hall for groups. The vaulted area once served as a wine-cellar. The cooking here is quite creative and to a high standard (menus start from approximately FF 120). The owners also run a wine estate (see below) and hotel-restaurant *Le Clos des Délices* in Ottrott.

BOERSCH

In the 12th century Boersch became the property of the archbishop of Strasbourg and remained so for centuries. In the 14th century it received ramparts, of which there remain three gateways and a few sections of the walls. Inside the gateways the winding streets run upwards to the cobbled courtyard on which the imposing town hall was built in the 16th century. Nearby there is an old well for six buckets and the Saint-Médard church. This dates, for the most part, from the 18th century, but a few frescos, as well as the church towers, are Romanesque. A stroll through tiny Boersch is visually very pleasing, because the village has numerous beautiful buildings. Twice a year there is a festival here: at the end of July and at the end of October.

One of Boersch's three gateways.

RECOMMENDED PRODUCERS
Hummel This family has been making wine since 1109. The cellars lie outside the old centre in the direction of Saint-Léonard.
Schaetzel Although the vineyards of this wine estate lie mainly in Ottrott and the family Schaetzel also has a tasting room

there, everything is vinified and bottled in Boersch. What's more, here they are geared to receive groups of wine lovers. The tasting room (dating from 1722, see *Le Châtelain* above) also contains a collection of old wine tools. The best wine is generally the Rouge d'Ottrott, Cuvée Châtelain.

OTTROTT

Despite its modest size, Ottrott, which is built against the foothills, has about ten hotels: people from Strasbourg and other cities like to seek their relaxation here. In a part of the village that lies lower down (Ottrott-le-Bas), the 12th century Saint-Nicolas chapel stands hidden behind

Rouge d'Ottrott is the local speciality.

houses. This grey building has been renovated many times and has a 16th century statue of the Virgin Mary. The parish church, with its Silbermann organ, is found in the higher situated Ottrott-le-Haut. In the direct vicinity of the church are various hotel-restaurants and tasting rooms. A short walk along the cobbled street is worth the trouble. In the surroundings of Ottrott are various castle ruins, such as those of Ratsamhausen and Lutzelbourg. Rouge d'Ottrott, a wine that can be red or rosé, has been a speciality here for generations.

HOTEL
Le Clos des Délices
✆ 88.95.81.00
A complex of six hectares situated peacefully in the countryside. It has 25 very comfortable rooms, a swimming pool and other facilities. Prices commence at around FF 400. The restaurant also has style.

RESTAURANTS
Ami Fritz
✆ 88.95.80.81
Warm ambience, nice service, regional specialities and reasonable menu prices. There is also a well-cared-for hotel.
Beau Site
✆ 88.95.80.61
A restaurant with a very high reputation and many game dishes in season (with which the Rouge d'Ottrott goes perfectly). Large wine list. Menus commence at approximately FF 100. There are also 15 excellent hotel rooms (two for non-smokers; most cost FF 400 to 500).

RECOMMENDED PRODUCERS
Fritz This belongs to the same family that owns *Ami Fritz* and the hotel annexe belonging to it. Among the better wines are Rouge d'Ottrott, Auxerrois and Gewurztraminer Affenberg.
Schaetzel See under Boersch.
Jean-Charles Vonville The cellars lie

on the crossroads in Ottrott-le-Bas. Very successful Rouge d'Ottrott, in particular the wood-matured type.

RELATED TO WINE
• At the end of August the festival of the Rouge d'Ottrott is celebrated: an opportunity to test the local red wines.

HOTELS

A la cour d'Alsace
℘ 88.95.07.00
Of the more than 15 hotels in Obernai, this is the most luxurious. It is situated near the centre, surrounding a courtyard, and is reached by means of an alley. Its more than 40 rooms are large and tastefully furnished. Prices run from FF 400. The hotel has a garden and a restaurant at its disposal.

Hostellerie La Diligence
℘ 88.95.55.69
Old-fashioned, chic rooms (24) on the market square. All rooms are different. Price about FF 300. The restaurant on the ground floor is not used by the hotel. Slightly to the west of the city centre are two more modern and more peaceful annexes: *Exquisit Résidence* and *Bel Air Résidence*.

Le Parc

The Kappelturm next to one of the hotels.

The place du Marché is the heart of the city.

OBERNAI

Obernai, which has almost 10,000 inhabitants, is one of the most important attractions of northern Alsace, and justly so because the city has much to offer. Its heart consists of the place du Marché, which is surrounded by half-timbered houses. Here where the beautiful Corn Exchange stands, is a building in Renaissance style, dating from 1554. Across from it, on the other side of the square, is the city hall. It dates from the 15th and 16th centuries but its decorated balcony was added as late as the 17th century. Directly next to the *hôtel de ville* rises the 72 metre high Kappelturm or chapel tower. At the foot of its spire are four, small, Gothic look-out towers. The lowest part of the tower is Romanesque. Only the choir of the chapel, which formerly stood beside the tower, remains. Two other spires can be seen behind the houses on the northern side of the market square.

RECOMMENDED PRODUCERS

Eugène Blanck & Fils A family wine estate with quite a lot of land in Obernai and its surroundings. Among the specialities are the Tokay Pinot Gris and the Rouge d'Ottrott. The cellars and the reasonably large reception room are situated near the hotel-restaurant *Le Parc*.

Cave d'Obernai Belongs to a group of wine cooperatives. The quality of the wines is frequently average, but sometimes the Gewurztraminer réserve and the Crémant can be pleasantly surprising. A well-known brand is Fritz Kobus.

Charmingly decorated well.

They belong to the church of Saint-Paul et Saint-Pierre, a piece of architecture built in the Gothic style and dating from the 19th century. On the way from the market square to the church one passes a wonderful stone well which is richly decorated. Nowadays, its six buckets are no longer filled with water but with geraniums.

The eastern side of the church is a good starting point for a walk along the ramparts. These consist of four parts which stretch around the centre of Obernai and are marked out by various towers. The walk could be interrupted at the rue du Général Gouraud. By turning to the right one soon arrives at the place de l'Etoile, a photogenic square with splendid houses and various timbered façades. One of the buildings has a multicoloured roof such as is often encountered in Burgundy. It is a short walk to the market square. It was once possible to park on the square but nowadays it has, as much as possible, been made free of cars. In summer there are horse-drawn carriages in which you can take a tour.

On the square itself Saint Odile is immortalized. She stands as a piece of sculpture above a foun-

✆ 88.95.50.08
A hotel-restaurant which has a very good reputation locally. Stylishly furnished rooms, 50 in total. They are also supplied with all conveniences, such as hairdriers. *Le Parc* also has at its disposal an outdoor and indoor swimming pool, a sauna, a solarium and other facilities. Most rooms cost FF 450 to 500. A visit to the dining room, with its beams and brown wainscotting is enjoyable: the food is delicious (menus from around FF 200), and the choice of digestives is impressive.

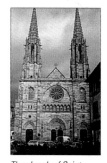

The church of Saint-Pierre et Saint-Paul.

Clos Sainte-Odile This property of about 10 hectares is walled and lies against a hill above Obernai. The planting consists of 50 per cent gewurztraminer, 25 per cent tokay pinot gris and 25 per cent riesling. In general the first two varieties offer the best wines. The Clos is used by the Cave d'Obernai.

Seilly This winegrower (established at number 18 on the rue Général Gouraud) makes a terrific Edelzwicker (baptized 'Vin du Pistolet'), while his Tokay Pinot Gris is, as a rule, not to be scorned.

RESTAURANT
L'Agneau d'Or
© 88.95.28.22
Winstub where, for surprisingly little money, one can eat unexpectedly well. Purely regional cuisine.

A museum is situated in the Corn Exchange.

TOURIST TIPS
• In the Corn Exchange a small museum has been established.
• In the direction of Saint-Léonard (not far from Boersch) the Musée du Cheval et de l'Attelage is situated. This Horse and Carriage Museum not only deserves attention for its collection, but also because it borders on two magnificent gardens in the French and Italian styles respectively. The museum is mainly open from July through September.

tain dating from the beginning of the 20th century. According to legend, Odile was born, blind and mentally defective, around the year 660, as the first child of Duke Etichon. The father was furious because he had wanted a son and gave orders to kill her. However, a wet nurse kept her alive. Later, at the age of twelve, Odile was baptized. At the same moment she gained her sight, her senses and beauty. After difficulties with her father, who wished to marry her off, a miracle occurred and a rock opened up so that she could hide herself. The duke admitted defeat and, on a mountain summit, he built a convent, of which Odile became abbess. This convent, Le Mont Sainte-Odile, still exists and yearly attracts thousands of visitors. The sarcophagus in which Odile lies buried rests in one of the four chapels; paintings and bas-reliefs show scenes depicting her life.

Obernai is not an important wine community due to the fact that it does not have even 100 hectares of grapevines. None the less, a famous vineyard is to be found here, towering over the roofs on the northern side – the Clos Sainte-Odile.

RELATED TO WINE
• The yearly wine exchange takes place on the second Sunday in October.
• On the wine hill above Obernai a sentier viticole is set out.

HOTEL
Relais du Klevener
© 88.08.05.98
After remaining empty
for years, this 32-room
hotel was reopened in
1988. Since then it has
been run by the wine-
growing family Meckert
(see below). The rooms
were entirely renovated
and almost all have a
shower and toilet.
Those on the eastern
side offer a spectacular
view over the Rhine val-
ley. Prices: FF 200 to
350. The restaurant is a
Brasserie where region-
al dishes are prepared
with care. This is also a
good address for a light
lunch (*pâté en croute,*
various salads). On Sat-
urday and Sunday even-
ings there is usually
tarte flambée.

HEILIGENSTEIN

From a recess high against the façade of Heiligen-
steins city hall the statue of Ehrhard Wantz stares
down. This is a trib-
ute to the man who
was the first to plant
the grape variety kle-
vener in this old wine
village. This took
place in 1742. The ex-
act origin of the kle-
vener is unknown,
but it is certain that
the variety is synony-
mous with the savag-
nin rose, also known
as traminer, rotedel or
edelrose. The experi-
ment by Wantz was

A statue of Ehrhard Wantz.

successful and a short time later klevener vines
yielded twice the amount of the ordinary vines.
In 1971 Klevener de Heiligenstein received its
own *appellation.* At present 20 to 30 hectares have
been planted with this rare grape. Its wine is
mild-fresh, firm, lightly spiced and full of character.

Modern Heiligenstein is a small village close to
Barr. Along the fairly narrow main street one
finds not only the town hall but also the 16th century Fountain of the Bear, who carries the village
coat of arms in his front paws. In front of the
fountain a Merovingian sarcophagus lies, dating

RECOMMENDED PRODUCERS
Heywang Small family wine estate
which makes exemplary wines, such as
Sylvaner, Tokay Pinot Gris, Muscat, Gewurztraminer Affenberg, Gewurztraminer
grand cru Kirchberg de Barr and Klevener
de Heiligenstein. All wines here are fermented in wooden casks.

René Meckert & Fils Active proprietors
of an average sized firm, and owners of
the Clos Schwendehiesel. Among the
most interesting wines are the Gewurztraminer of the walled vineyard already
mentioned and the Klevener de Heiligenstein. The family also owns the hotel-restaurant Relais du Klevener.

The 16th century Fountain of the Bear.

from the 8th century. This was carved from a single piece of pink sandstone from the Vosges. Although the local church is Romanesque in origin, this style is only found in the lower part of the towers. In and around Heiligenstein there are no less than six walking circuits. The walk along the Klevener vineyards lasts one and a half hours. A lovely panorama can be enjoyed at various places in the village, because Heiligenstein is built on the last foothill before the Rhine plain.

RESTAURANT
Au Raisin d'Or
✆ 88.08.95.23
A rural inn with a lot of brown and red in the interior. There is a nice three-course menu for approximately FF 100. Delicious *truite au Riesling*

A. Ruff & Fils Small producers with good Klevener de Heiligenstein.

RELATED TO WINE
• Klevener de Heiligenstein is brought on the market by, among others, the wine merchants of Charles Wantz – the founder of which was related to the klevener pioneer Ehrhard Wantz – and Willm, both in Barr. Another producer from outside the community of Heiligenstein is the cooperative of Andlau, which is also located in Barr.
• The Fête du Klevener usually takes place on the second Sunday in August.

BARR

Coming from Heiligenstein, one drives into Barr along the slope of a hill which, at a certain point,

In the garden of Willm.

is planted on the left side with grapevines; behind this a large portion of the city can be seen. The vineyard is called Clos de la Folie Marco and produces a delicious Sylvaner. On the other side of the street are the premises of the wine house Willm (which also deals in snails) and the Musée de la Folie Marco. The latter is a mansion containing Alsatian furniture dating from the 17th to the 19th century. In the cellar under the museum is a simple restaurant. Next to the museum – which also has a nice garden – runs a narrow street leading to the local *sentier viticole*. If the route is followed on after the museum, one passes a number of winegrowers' houses before arriving at the cobbled town hall square.

The *hôtel de ville* itself is a large, fine-looking building. It dates from 1640 and stands on the site of the former Kleppernburg castle. Half-way through July, Barr celebrates its wine exchange on

The harvest festival in Barr is in early October.

RECOMMENDED PRODUCERS
Hering Well over half of the nine hectares that Pierre and Lilian Hering own lies on the grand cru Kirchberg but the non-classified wines also have a lot of quality. Recommended are the Sylvaner Clos de la Folie Marco, Riesling Kirchberg, Muscat Feyel, Gewurztraminer

Kirchberg and Gewurztraminer Gaensbrunnel.
Klipfel A dynamic wine merchant that owns a few dozen hectares of property. These also give the best wines, such as the Gewurztraminer Clos Zisser, the Riesling and Gewurztraminer Kirchberg, the Gewurztraminer and Tokay Pinot Gris Frei-

Enjoying wine and tarte flambée during the annual wine exchange.

and around the large inner courtyard. This has existed since 1906 and is thus the oldest in Alsace. During the exchange over 300 wines from the surrounding area can be tasted in the rooms of the city hall. The *cour* is filled with tables and benches, *tarte flambée* can be eaten and dance groups perform regularly. Across from the city hall a fountain can be found and, diagonally behind, stands the (Protestant) church of Saint-Martin. It has a clock tower which is partially 12th century. In former times, the inhabitants sought refuge from acts of war in the fortified churchyard. The rest of the centre consists of a jumble of winding streets, where you can very easily lose your way.

RESTAURANTS
Hôtel de la Couronne
℡ 88.08.25.83
As far as cuisine is concerned, this is a rising star, thanks to a cuisine in which regional ingredients are inventively cooked (menus from approximately FF 75). It is situated near the city hall and also has a few simple rooms.

berg. The wood-matured Rouge de Barr also deserves attention. For the reception of tourists the firm has at its disposal a perfectly furnished reception room where much old wine equipment has been set out, including about 15 antique wine-presses.
Charles Stoeffler In the 17th century

cellar the Pinot Noir undergoes ageing in casks. Good Riesling.
Charles Wantz Average-sized wine merchant with, as its specialities, Riesling Wiebelsberg, Gewurztraminer, Klevener de Heiligenstein and Rouge d'Ottrott. It also bottles the wines of Château d'Ittenwiller.

Maison Rouge
☎ 88.08.90.40
In this large, reddish
half-timbered building
there is a brasserie, a
speciality restaurant
and a hotel with 13
rooms all furnished with
care (around FF 250).
The cuisine offers, for
very reasonable prices,
both traditional and
more modern dishes.
Cosy, somewhat rustic
interior and a terrace

Clos de la Folie Marco.

On the southern side
of the centre runs the
avenue des Vosges, a
broad street that
leads to the moun-
tains, and Mont
Sainte-Odile (see
Obernai). At a cross-
ing in this avenue
one turns off towards
Mittelbergheim, the
next location on the
wine route.

The many stately
buildings – which of-
ten have inner courtyards and gardens – give Barr
a prosperous look. Since olden times the local
economy has blossomed thanks to the river Kir-
neck (in whose valley Barr lies), the vineyards and
the nearby forests. Light industry , such as
leatherware, began in the 19th century. It still exists, while the wine trade is also important.

Aside from this, Barr stimulates tourism: in few
Alsatian communities do so many activities take
place as here. The season runs from the 1st of
May until late in December. Usually Barr has
4500 inhabitants; in the summer 1000 more
arrive.

The most important vineyard is the Kirchberg de
Barr, a grand cru. On clear days there is a wonderful panoramic view from this high field, sometimes even as far as the cathedral of Strasbourg.
Other reputed vineyards are Clos Zisser, Clos

Willm The name Willm is found on,
among others, such highly reputed wines
as Gewurztraminer Clos Gaensbrunnel,
Riesling Kirchberg de Barr and Tokay Pinot Gris, while Cuvée Emile Willm appears on, among others, Gewurztraminer
and Crémant and tasty Pinot Blanc Cordon
d'Alsace. The majority of shares belongs

to the cooperative of Eguisheim.

RELATED TO WINE
• The yearly wine exchange takes place
  on and around the 14th of July and lasts
  about five days.
• The harvest festival is at the beginning
  of October.

The Alsatian costume is also worn in Barr.

Gaensbrunnel (behind the cellars of Willm and named after the goose fountain in front of the Musée de la Folie Marco) and Freiberg. Barr's most successful type of wine is, in general, the Gewurztraminer.

TOURIST TIPS

- In July and August the Syndicat d'Initiative organizes guided walks and visits to wine cellars as well as the museum.
- In the summer there are regular concerts in the Protestant church and elsewhere.
- On the Blossberg, above Barr, a remnant of a Celtic wall is to be found.

The Boeckel wine tavern and Gilg Winstub.

MITTELBERGHEIM

While the neighbouring communities of Barr and Andlau grew up in valleys, Mittelbergheim was built on a hill. Originally a Frankish settlement, it blossomed in the 16th century when hard-working Protestant families, who had fled Andlau for religious reasons, settled here. Most houses in the village date from this century or the following one. Almost all of them line the two narrow streets that cross each other on the hilltop, near the hotel-restaurant Gilg and the city hall. The city hall, which is a 17th century building, has a striking cupola supported by pillars above its outside staircase. Of the two churches, the Protestant one is the older and more beautiful, thanks to Romanesque and Gothic elements. Many of the well-preserved buildings are decorated with ornaments and one frequently sees the symbols of winegrowers because, for many centuries here, wine has been an important source of income. Mittelbergheim also calls itself

The Protestant church.

HOTEL
Winstub Gilg
℃ 88.08.91.37
Hotel-restaurant with 10 simple rooms surrounding an inner courtyard (FF 200 to 300). In the rustically furnished restaurant the cooking is good; both traditional as well as more refined dishes taste excellent here. There is a choice of many local and other wines.

RESTAURANT
Am Lindeplätzel
℃ 88.08.10.69
A relatively new establishment where, for reasonable prices (menus start at less than FF 100 and run to about FF 200), quite fine dishes are offered. The *patron* himself cooks.

RECOMMENDED PRODUCERS
E.Boeckel Medium-sized wine merchant The wines are full of character, such as the Sylvaner Vieilles Vignes, the Riesling and the Gewurztraminer from the Zotzenberg, the Riesling Wiebelsberg and the Riesling Brandluft.
Paul Brandner Aromatic Sylvaner

Zotzenberg.
Christian Dolder Tasty Sylvaner Zotzenberg and Riesling Brandluft.
Armand Gilg & Fils One of the most trend-setting and largest wine estates of the village. In the range one finds, among others, a fine Muscat.
Julien Rieffel & Fils Delivers wine with

Country road through the Zotzenberg vineyard.

'La cité du vin' and, along the rue de la Montagne, a 17th century winepress stands under a lean-to.

The most famous vineyard of Mittelbergheim is the grand cru Zotzenberg, which lies directly to the northwest of the village. Here a *sentier viticole* is set out. The field produces superior Sylvaners, but because this type of wine can never be *grand cru*, the sylvaner is being increasingly replaced, mostly by riesling and gewurztraminer.

a good average quality, such as the Riesling and Sylvaner Zotzenberg, Tokay Pinot Gris Kirchberg, Muscat and Klevener.
Rietsch Pierre and Jean-Pierre Rietsch offer a Muscat Zotzenberg.
A. Seltz & Fils Serious wine merchant. A number of successful wines: Sylvaner Zotzenberg, Clevener, Muscat, Gewurz-

traminer Zotzenberg and Riesling (the top quality Réserve and Réserve Particulière).
Emile Seltz A wine estate that believes in Sylvaner and also mainly produces it.

RELATED TO WINE
- The annual wine festival generally takes place in the last weekend of July.

HOTEL
Kastelberg
© 88.08.97.83
Quite modern hotel at
the foot of the vineyard
of the same name, along
the road to Mittelber-
gheim. The 30 rooms are
functionally furnished.
Prices are around FF 300.

ANDLAU

It was around the year 880 that Empress Richarde left her husband Charlemagne in order to devote herself to cultural and spiritual affairs in the region of her birth. At the place where she settled, in the valley of the Andlau, a convent arose with the village of Andlau surrounding it. Richarde

Richarde stands next to the Au Boeuf Rouge.

was later canonized. One of her statues stands above a fountain in the city hall square and her crypt is situated in the convent church. The church was rebuilt late in the 17th century and early in the 18th century, but still has Romanesque elements. The eastern side, for example, is decorated with an almost 30 metre long frieze with sculpted fantastic animals and

RESTAURANTS
Au Boeuf Rouge
© 88.08.96.26
This family business is
located in a building
dating from 1546. The
dining room gives a
warm, cosy impression.
Alsatian specialities and
personal creations are
all made with care. Me-
nus start from FF 150.
One can adjourn to the
salon for small dishes.

other images. The Romanesque portal is also richly decorated. The church has a Gothic nave and contains innumerable religious works of art. On the eastern side of the village, in the direction of Itterswiller, the chapel of Saint-André stands against a slope. The clock towers, and probably also the frescos, date from the 15th century. The actual village is an extremely pleasant spot, with winding streets and many half-timbered houses. In the neighbourhood of Andlau, the ruins of the castles of Andlau and Spesbourg are to be found. That of Andlau is the more impressive, with two round castle towers and Gothic window openings.

RECOMMENDED PRODUCERS
André Durrmann The best wine is the Riesling Wiebelsberg, followed by the Riesling Kastelberg. A small wine estate.
Domaine André et Rémy Gresser The son, Rémy is a talented wine maker. His Rieslings have a lot of personality, such as the Kastelberg, Moenchberg and Wie-

belsberg. Also worth discovering are the Andlau Sylvaner, Muscat Andlau-Brand-hof and Kritt-Gewurztraminer.
Marc Kreydenweiss Makes a series of striking wines, among others the Klevner Kritt, Muscat Clos Rebgarten, Tokay Pinot Gris Moenchberg, Gewurztraminer Kritt, Clos du Val and the Rieslings of Kastel-

A view of Andlau and the chapel of Saint-André.

Le Relais de la Poste
© 88.08.95.91
Sympathetic *winstub*, where mainly regional dishes are served. They are pleasant and reasonably priced.

TOURIST TIPS
- At the junction outside Andlau, where one turns right towards Itterswiller, stands the so-called 'Bank of the King of Rome'. This royal domicile has walls and a roof and is made from blocks of red sandstone.
- In the crypt and also next to the statues of St. Richarde there are sculptures of she-bears. They are connected with a legend in which an angel apparently advised the empress to settle on the spot where a bear dug a hole – that was in the Andlau valley.

Inside the municipal boundaries of Andlau lie three vineyards with grand cru status: Kastelberg, Moenchberg and Wiebelsberg. Above all, their Rieslings enjoy a good name.

berg, Moenchberg and Wiebelsberg.
Robert Mattern et Fils Taste the Rieslings of Moenchberg and Wiebelsberg here, as well as the Gewurztraminer Kusterhof.
Guy Wach/Domaine des Maronniers
Quality conscious *vigneron*. Sylvaner, Tokay Pinot Gris, Riesling Kastelberg.

RELATED TO WINE
- On the initiative of Rémy Gresser, the wine fraternity La Confrérie des Hospitaliers du Haut d'Andlau has, a number of times, organized 'the Day of the Grands Crus'. Usually the event takes place in May.

Itterswiller stretches out over the crest of a hill.

HOTEL
Arnold
℃ 88.85.50.58
The Arnold family also
has a popular winstub in
Itterswiller but the
buildings stand apart
from each other. What's
more, the restaurant is
rustically furnished and
the hotel (divided
between two buildings)
without caprices, in
light tones. Prices
around FF 450.

IN AND AROUND ITTERSWILLER

After passing a wine plateau, Itterswiller comes
into sight. This is a beautiful village of Roman
origin, which lies on a hill. It consists of not
much more than an extended main street and fe-
wer than 300 people live here. It is therefore remarkable that Itterswiller has four hotels, of
which three have a restaurant. The reason that the
village attracts so many visitors is the marvellous
view to the south and the well-cared-for impres-
sion that it gives. In summer most of the houses
are decorated with a wealth of flowers. Under the
clock tower is a chapel with many Romanesque
frescos.

RECOMMENDED PRODUCERS
ITTERSWILLER
François Kieffer & Fils A firm Gewurz-
traminer. Attractive Crémant.
Justin Schwartz Exquisite wines, among
which Tokay Pinot Gris and Pinot Noir.
EPFIG
Patrick Beyer Sylvaner, Pinot Blanc, Ge-

wurztraminer, Pinot Noir Rosé.
André Ostertag A self-willed winegrow-
er with much talent. Sylvaner Vieilles
Vignes, Pinot Blanc, Muscat and Riesling
Fronholz, Riesling and Tokay Pinot Gris
Muenchberg, Riesling Heissenberg, etc.
NOTHALTEN
Gérard Landmann Makes, among oth-

From Itterswiller it is only a few kilometres to Epfig. This colourless village is plagued by much traffic, but has an interesting monument: the chapel of Sainte-Marguerite. This is situated at the end of a street which runs, with a right-angled turn, in an easterly direction. The oldest part of the chapel dates from the beginning

Arnold winstub and its shop.

of the 11th century. Later extensions were made, such as the Romanesque arcade.

By returning to Itterswiller one arrives once more on the wine route. Left, the road runs down to

Gravestone at the chapel Sainte-Marguerite in Epfig.

Nothalten, where the winding main street has a number of colourful houses and an octagonal Renaissance fountain dating from 1543. It stands on the village square. The fact that Blienschwiller, the next village, profits mainly from wine is shown by the signs and barrels that have been installed on practically all the buildings.

RESTAURANT
Winstub Arnold
℃ 88.85.50.58
Large restaurant, divided among three rooms in a half-timbered house, which, until October, is decorated with flowers. Nutritious, tasty dishes, prepared with a feeling for tradition. Menus from approximately FF 200 (more expensive on Sunday). Unfortunately, the wines from their own wine estate – Arnold Simon – are not brilliant.

TOURIST TIPS
• Winstub Arnold has a nice gift shop.
• The clock tower of Blienschwiller is part Romanesque.

ers, a Riesling Muenchberg.
Julien Meyer This is a local favourite, thanks to wines such as Muscat Petite Fleur, Riesling Muenchberg.
BLIENSCHWILLER
Marc Auther Specialize in Rieslings, which taste extremely fine.
Cave de la Dîme Specialities: Riesling

Réserve de la Dîme, Gewurztraminer Winzenberg and a wood-matured Pinot Noir.
René Kientz Has a good name due to his Crémant and many other wines.
E.Spitz & Fils The Muscat is very tasty.

RELATED TO WINE
• Epfig has a wine promenade.

DAMBACH-LA-VILLE

HOTELS
Au Raisin d'Or
✆ 88.92.40.08
Rural establishment
with simply furnished,
neat rooms. Prices:
FF 200 to 250. In the
restaurant, decorated
with much woodwork,
chiefly regional dishes
are served.
Le Vignoble
✆ 88.92.43.75
Intimate, small hotel in
an old building next to
the church. Seven
rooms, all different.
Prices: FF 220 to 300.
Opened in 1991.

RESTAURANTS
A l'Arbre Vert
✆ 88.92.42.75
Simple eating-house
close to the northern
gateway. *Choucroute,
baekoffe, tarte flambée*,
and suchlike.
Tearoom Kamm
✆ 88.92.40.65
Established in a pastry
shop and ideal for a late
breakfast or afternoon
tea (large selection).
Fresh croissants, *kugel-
hopf*, pastries and tasty
pies.

The city hall.

Whoever enters
Dambach-la-Ville
through one of the
three middle-age
entry towers immedi-
ately experiences the
charm of this well-
preserved city. There
are many half-timbe-
red houses and other
old buildings. On
various occasions,
Dambach has won
the annual competi-
tion of the *villes et
villages fleuris*. A fine group is formed by the
slightly sloping city hall square. The *hôtel de ville*
(1547) has a stepped gable, next door rises a powerful half-timbered building (Hôtel de la Couronne, dating from 1569) and across from it one

The partially Romanesque chapel of Saint-Sébastien.

RECOMMENDED PRODUCERS
Pierre Arnold Crowned ordinary Rie-
sling. Excellent Riesling Frankstein.
Jean-Claude Beck Pinot Blanc, Riesling
Frankstein and Gewurztraminer Fronholtz,
among others.
Laurent Dietrich & Fils Riesling, Ge-
wurztraminer, Pinot Blanc, Pinot Noir.

Jean-Louis Dirringer Exquisite
Crémant, delicious Muscat.
Louis Gisselbrecht Riesling Frankstein,
Edelzwicker, Sylvaner and Pinot Blanc.
Willy Gisselbrecht & Fils Successful
wines. Examples: Auxerrois, Pinot Blanc,
Riesling Frankstein.
J.Hauller & Fils Some great wines, such

TOURIST TIPS
- Apart from his cellars, Louis Hauller has opened a gift shop. There, he sells CDs by the orchestra that he conducts, Les Joyeux Vignerons de Dambach-la-Ville.

The Hôtel de la Couronne, a half-timbered building.

encounters the Fountain of the Bear (1542). The city was formerly called Dambach-*la-Vigne* and nowadays has the largest area of vineyards in the whole department of Bas-Rhin, approximately 500 hectares. In the middle of the vineyards stands, slightly to the northwest of the embankments, the chapel of Saint-Sébastien. This monument, with its white walls, is in part Romanesque. The choir has Gothic windows and the retable is a Baroque masterpiece dating from the end of the 17th century. In the artistic woodcarving one sees the Virgin Mary in Alsatian costume.

The church stands next to the Frankstein, the grand cru of Dambach. Through the same land runs, from the city hall square, a *sentier viticole* (duration approximately one and a half hours). As the best wines of the Frankstein count the Riesling and Gewurztraminer.

as the Riesling and Gewurztraminer Cuvée Saint-Sébastien.

Louis Hauller/Domaine du Tonnelier Fine wines, such as Klevner, Riesling, Riesling Frankstein, Riesling Fronholtz, Riesling Winzenberg, Gewurztraminer Frankstein and Pinot Noir.

Ruhlmann-Dirringer Wines full of character: Sylvaner (litre bottle), an alluring Muscat and a noble Riesling Frankstein.

Schaeffer-Woerly Exquisite Pinot Blanc, Muscat and Riesling Frankstein.

RELATED TO WINE
- In the first half of August Dambach celebrates the Fête du Vin (estab. 1964).

HOTEL
Les Châteaux
✆ 88.92.49.13
Large hotel that was
opened in November
1991. It is situated just
outside Dieffenthal, in
the midst of vineyards.
Over 30 bright rooms, al-
ways with a good view.
Prices around FF 350.
Besides the usual res-
taurant, the business
also has a bar, and win-
stub (small menu, *chou-
croute au Riesling* and
the like) and an under-
ground *caveau* (*tarte
flambée*).

RESTAURANT
Winstub à
l'Ortenbourg
✆ 88.92.06.37
Unpretentious restau-
rant, property of the
winegrowing Dussourt
family in Scherwiller:
*pâté fermier, filet de
truite*, salads, entrecôte
and, in the evening,
tarte flambée.

The winstub called à l'Ortenbourg.

IN AND AROUND SCHERWILLER

Just off the wine route, the village of Dieffenthal
lies surrounded by vineyards. Due to its sheltered

*A 17th century sentry post above
a stream.*

location, there is a
somewhat warmer
microclimate here,
which makes the
grapes ripen earlier.
The Baroque church
is 18th century. Di-
rectly after Dieffen-
thal the wine hills
stop and the land-
scape becomes flat
and boring. Then
Scherwiller comes
into sight. The *route
du vin* proceeds at
right angles through

RECOMMENDED PRODUCERS
SCHERWILLER
André Dussourt Enterprising wine-
grower, who owns a wine estate, and a
tabac as well as a neighbouring winstub.
He makes 20 different wines. The best in-
clude his Riesling and Gewurztraminer
Réserve Prestige, both repeatedly

crowned. His Sylvaner, Pinot Blanc and
Tokay Pinot Gris also tend to taste good.
Robert Haag Racy Riesling Ortenberg.
CHATENOIS
Bernhard Reibel A wine estate run by
Cécile Bernhard, with cellars in the street
running parallel with the main street. Rie-
sling Weingarten, Tokay Pinot Gris Cuvée

it, but runs through a totally uninteresting street. It is therefore better to drive into the centre as soon as possible. Many half-timbered buildings are situated there, including a 17th century sentry post. This can be found, standing apart beside a stream which flows through Scherwiller via mini-canals. It separates many houses from the street and is consequently spanned by small pedestrian bridges.

In the vicinity of Scherwiller are found the castle ruins of Ortenbourg and Ramstein. More than two-thirds of the vineyards are planted with riesling. As a result, Le Confrérie des Rieslinger was founded in 1980. Having crossed the Giessen from Scherwiller, one soon arrives in Châtenois, whose main street has old buildings on both sides (including the city hall dating from 1493) and is so broad that it looks like a square. One side contains the tower gateway of the Witches. The church not only has an unusual clock tower (multicoloured spire with four wooden corner turrets), but also an organ by Silbermann and superb woodcarvings.

One of the small canals.

TOURIST TIP
- Close to Scherwiller, in 1525, the last battle between 26,000 rebellious peasants and the far better armed mercenaries of the duke of Lotharingen took place. The peasants met a bloody defeat. A cross near the Giessen (to the south of the village) serves as a remembrance.

de la Saint-Hubert.
Gilbert Dontenville It is certainly worth a visit, if only for his Riesling Hahnenberg.

RELATED TO WINE
- A parade, a trade market, tasting stands and music are a few of the elements of the event Art, Artisanat, Riesling, which

Scherwiller celebrates annually on the Sunday after August 15.
- Two *sentiers viticoles* have been laid out through the vineyards, one is two, and the other six, kilometres long. In summer, on Fridays, one can follow the longer with a guide and taste wine at the end.

A place to dine.

RESTAURANT
Auberge Saint-Martin
℡ 88.82.04.78
A cosy place to eat along the main street of Kintzheim. A number of tables stand in a covered porch. Nicely priced menus. One of the most popular dishes is *tarte flambée*.

NEAR HAUT-KOENIGSBOURG

The most famous silhouette of Alsace is that of the castle of Haut-Koenigsbourg, a giant bulwark situated on a 755 metre high mountain peak. The fortress was built at the beginning of the 20th century on the foundations of a castle ruin; its patron was German emperor Wilhelm II. The structure was declared a monument by the French government and is nowadays a large public attraction. As long as the top is not veiled by clouds, one has a sublime view from Haut-Koenigsbourg. Many tourists pass Kintzheim on the way to the castle. This town (not to be confused with Kientzheim) has taken advantage of this by developing a number of attractions. On La Montagne des Singes 300 apes run loose in a wildlife park of 20 hectares. The animals can be fed by hand. In La Volerie des Aigles demonstrations with birds of prey are given at the foot of the castle ruins. Finally, there is the Parc des

Near the castle entrance.

The mighty fortress of Haut-Koenigsbourg.

RECOMMENDED PRODUCERS
KINTZHEIM
Jean-Marie Koehly Makes wood-matured Pinot Noir.
ORSCHWILLER
Claude Bléger This wine estate, which operates without herbicides, has received many awards for its wines: Sylvaner, Pinot Blanc, Riesling, Tokay Pinot Gris, Gewurztraminer, Pinot Noir.
Cooperative Orschwiller-Kintzheim Since 1983 this business has produced a series of nice wines under the brand name Les Faîtières. Try the Riesling.
Raymond Engel A rather large wine estate with very trustworthy wines, such as

In the centre of Orschwiller.

Cigognes et des Loisirs, a small amusement park, as well as a zoo. Wine is also made in Kintzheim; this is indicated by the signs along the main street and the giant bottle of Riesling at the northern entry. The village has some half-timbered houses, some with a stork's nest.

Just past Kintzheim, the dome-shaped clock tower of Orschwiller's partially Baroque, pink church rises up. In this wine village without pavements, one can follow a small *circuit pittoresque*.

TOURIST TIPS

- Near Kintzheim's castle ruin (where demonstrations with birds of prey take place) stands a 15th century chapel.
- Near the church in Orschwiller there is a fine view across the Rhine plain. Near the city hall stands a (quite recent) wooden statue of a smith.

Riesling, Gewurztraminer and Crémant.
Domaine Siffert Excellent Riesling Prae-latenberg, Gewurztraminer, Pinot Noir.
A.Zimmermann Fils Makes a Tokay Pinot Gris that is occasionally special, and a Riesling Cuvée Geneviève that is always aromatic.

RELATED TO WINE

- In Orschwiller the winegrower Paul Fahrer has a small Musée du Vigneron.
- Around the 15th of August, Orschwiller celebrates its wine festival. Wine can be tasted in all the cellars .
- The grand cru of Kintzheim and Orschwiller is the Praelatenberg.

HOTEL
Aux Ducs de Lorraine
℡ 89.73.00.09
Large hotel and restaurant complex, consisting of various buildings and wings. In 1988 the rooms were renovated. They are stylishly and comfortably furnished. Different price ranges (from FF 400 up to FF 1100 for an apartment). Spacious, cosy dining room decorated with wood. Substantial, regionally oriented cuisine with game when in season. Menus from approximately FF 100 to FF 300. The wines come from their private family wine estate, Alsace Munsch (managed by René Meyer).

Ancient watch tower of Saint-Hippolyte.

THE NORTHERN HAUT-RHIN

Slightly south of Orschwiller lies the border between the two Alsatian departments Bas-Rhin and Haut-Rhin. The northernmost wine village of the Haut-Rhin is Saint-Hippolyte, of which the old centre, which is square, was fortified in the 13th century by the duke of Lotharingen. Parts of the fortifications still remain, including a large, round corner tower.

The wine route runs in a right-angled bend through the village. At this corner there stands a fine *mairie*, dating from 1792 and, behind it, a small square (half-timbered houses, fountain) and the 14th century parish church. Inside are frescos from 1904, a Silbermann organ from 1738, a Gothic

A statue in Saint-Hippolyte.

RECOMMENDED PRODUCERS
SAINT-HIPPOLYTE
Huber Bléger Coming from Orschwiller, at a bend on the right, the road passes a grey chapel. The cellars of Huber Bléger, a wine estate worked by two families, are situated there. Clevner, Pinot Noir.
Jacques Iltis High-quality wines, such

as Rouge de Saint-Hippolyte and Riesling Schlossreben.
René Klein & Fils Modest wine estate with, among others, a good Riesling Schlossreben (Sélection René Klein).
Klein aux Vieux Remparts It is run by two oenologists, Jean-Marie and Françoise Klein. Top wines are the Riesling and

lectern and the relics of Saint Hippolytus (Roman martyr, 3rd century). Various houses in this charming village are decorated with wrought-iron corner posts; for eample, a building near the church.

The wine speciality is Rouge de Saint-Hippolyte, originating from the pinot noir. The same grape variety is processed in abundance in bordering Rodern, a quiet hamlet surrounded by wine hills, with sloping streets and a lot of atmosphere. In

Fountain in Saint-Hippolyte.

Gewurztraminer Schlossreben, Tokay Pinot Gris Geisberg, Rouge de Saint-Hippolyte (sometimes matured in new vats).
Muller-Koeberlé Rouge de Saint-Hippolyte, Riesling Burgreben. Good wine estate.

RODERN
Koeberlé-Klein A quality wine estate

with excellent Pinot Noir and Tokay Pinot Gris Gloeckelberg.
Charles Koehly & Fils Located on the rue du Pinot Noir. Clean, balanced wines, such as Riesling Saint-Hippolyte, Tokay Pinot Gris Gloeckelberg, Gewurztraminer Altenberg de Bergheim, Crémant.

The village of Rodern against the background of the Rhine plain.

Rodern there are numerous houses dating from the 16th century; the choir of the church is 15th century. Back on the *route du vin*, the roofs of Rohrschwihr soon come into sight. This is a friendly, but inconspicuous, wine village with a few fountains and a narrow, pointed church tower.

Half-timbered houses in Rodern.

RORSCHWIHR
Rolly Gassmann Large wine estate, friendly people, soft, exquisite wines. In the range are, among others, Sylvaner, various Rieslings (such as Pflaenzrereben, Silberberg), Muscat Moenchreben, Gewurztraminer (a few qualities), Auxerrois, Tokay Pinot Gris, Pinot Noir.

RELATED TO WINE
- On the third Sunday of September, Saint-Hippolyte celebrates the Fête du Vin Nouveau.
- The annual wine festival of Rodern is on the third or fourth Sunday of July.
- Saint-Hippolyte and Rodern have a joint Crand Cru, Gloeckelberg.

BERGHEIM

The Porte Haute, through which one drives into Bergheim, bears the date 1300, but older still is the lime tree in front of it because Bergheim celebrated its first *fête populaire* under it in the same year. The Porte Haute is not the only fortified gateway in this village, because the church is surrounded by the remains of moats and ramparts with, in total, nine defensive towers. A walking route has been laid out upon the walls. Bergheim's large city hall (1776), built of red sandstone, stands on a charming, cobbled market square with a fountain dating from the Baroque period and small trees.

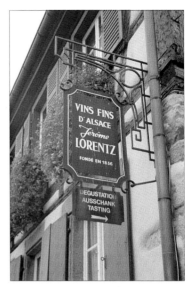

Wine tasting is also possible here.

The weekly market is held here on Mondays. The Notre-Dame church (likewise built of sandstone)

The market square, with the Porte Haute in the background.

The Porte Haute dates from 1300.

RECOMMENDED PRODUCERS

Domaine Marcel Deiss A family wine estate run dynamically by Jean-Michel Deiss. It has around 20 hectares, which, in Alsace, is a lot. The extensive range contains only high-quality wines, such as Edelzwicker, Sylvaner, Pinot Blanc, Muscat, Pinot Noir, Riesling and Gewurztra-

miner Altenberg de Bergheim, Riesling Schoenenbourg, Riesling Engelgarten, Riesling Grasberg.

Gustave Lorentz Since the 1980s, the quality of the wines has improved strikingly. Among the very best are the Riesling and Gewurztraminer Altenberg de Bergheim and the Riesling and Gewurz-

dates from 1347 but was largely rebuilt in the 18th century. The portal and the choir, however, have remained Gothic. On both sides of the church there are the cellars of wine producers.

If one follows the rue des Vignerons, which runs parallel with the Grand'Rue, you will pass old houses and also a couple of old fountains. Bergheim once enjoyed a curious privilege, namely that criminals were free from prosecution within the village walls. Witches and sorcerers were, on the contrary, not welcome: they were tortured in the Tour des Sorcières.

Bergheim owns a couple of grands crus, Altenberg and Kanzlerberg. They give excellent Gewurztraminers and Rieslings.

An excellent place for lunch and dinner.

HOTEL
Du Parc
☎ 89.73.63.07
Simple, country hotel. The 15 rooms, with their rather small beds, have been modernized and now contain telephone, TV, mini-bar and shower/bath plus toilet. Prices around FF 250. Always ask for a room at the rear to avoid noisy traffic: *Du Parc* lies along the wine route. In the old-fashioned, simple dining room you can eat a decent lunch quite cheaply (*feuilleté au Munster* with seasonal salads).

RESTAURANT
Winstub du Sommelier
☎ 89.73.69.99
Excellent for lunch and dinner. Strictly regional dishes are reasonably priced. It is the property of a former wine-waiter of Auberge de l'Ill so they have a large selection of wines and a number of them are served by the glass. Cosy interior with much wood.

traminer Kanzlerberg, but the Pinot Blanc, Muscat and Riesling Cuvée Particulière also tend to taste delicious. One of the secondary brands is Jérôme Lorentz.
Jean-Martin Spielmann Owns a lot of land in both grands crus and produces Gewurztraminer Altenberg, Riesling and Gewurztraminer Kanzlerberg. The Spiel-

mann cellars are situated outside the village centre, some dozen metres from the Porte Haute, in the direction of Thannenkirch.

RELATED TO WINE
• Next to the Domaine Marcel Deiss a *sentier viticole* begins.

The main street.

On the first Sunday of September, the streets of Ribeauvillé are usually almost filled to bursting, as the city celebrates its Pfifferdaj or Fête des Ménétriers. Street musicians, brass bands, decorated wagons and the King of the Minstrels roam through the streets; there is dancing, eating and drinking. The Renaissance fountain in front of the city hall even spurts wine (and is locally referred to as the Fontaine du Vin).

Pfifferdaj is a centuries-old tradition. After Ribeauvillé had been the property of the duke of Lotharingen, the counts of Eguisheim and the archbishop of Basel, respectively, it came into the possession of the counts of Ribeaupierre. They considered themselves the protectors and patrons

HOTELS
Le Ménestrel
℗ 89.73.80.52
Opened in 1989, it stands at a right angle to the road to Hunawihr. Colourful, cheerful rooms, with tiny balconies on the first floor. Sauna, jacuzzi, turkish bath, tea room. Prices: FF 400 to 450.
Les Seigneurs de Ribeaupierre
℗ 89.73.70.31
A hotel full of atmosphere in a 17th century building beside the Grand'Rue. Only six rooms (from FF 400) and four suites (from FF 500).
La Tour
℗ 89.73.72.73
Next to the city hall (and close to a clock tower which chimes frequently). Tidy, simple rooms with floors that often creak. Prices: FF 300 to 400.

Near Ribeauvillé there are three castle ruins.

RECOMMENDED PRODUCERS
Bott Fréres Small wine merchant with generally elegant wines. The highest qualities are represented by the title Cuvée Exceptionnelle. Among these the Muscat, Riesling, Tokay Pinot Gris and Gewurztraminer are remarkable.
Cooperative Ribeauvillé has the oldest wine cooperative of France, founded in 1895. The business has modern equipment and makes a series of attractive wines. The Pinot Blanc tends to be very successful, as is the Pinot Noir. High up on the list one finds the Rieslings of Kirchberg and Osterberg, as well as the Clos du Zahnacker made from various

of all minstrels and, consequently, commencing in 1715, ministrels flocked to Ribeauvillé to play for the counts and the inhabitants. The musicians resided in the Auberge du Soleil on the place de la Sinn. This building, with its round towers and covered balcony, still exists, but no longer serves as an inn.

The 13th century Butchers tower.

Reminders of the counts of Ribeaupierre are seen in the three ruins of the castles where they lived: Saint-Ulrich (the largest), Girsberg and Haut-Ribeaupierre.

It is not only on Pfifferdaj that Ribeauvillé deserves a visit. On the eastern side stand two fortified towers with storks' nests. Near them the Grand'Rue begins, the long, narrow main street that runs past nearly all the monuments – and contains numerous nice shops. First, one walks past a fountain with a small statue of a winegrower and the renowned hotel-restaurant *Des Vosges*, with the wine tavern Louis Sipp across from it. Not much further, on the right side of the street, is the Zum Pfifferhüs winstub. This has a half-timbered façade with beautiful woodwork, which depicts the Annunciation. After that comes the Gothic Corn Exchange with a double portal.

RESTAURANT
Auberge de l'Illhausern
☎ 89.71.83.23
One of France's – and therefore one of the world's – best restaurants, a 15 minute drive from Ribeauvillé. Three stars in the *Guide Michelin* and corresponding prices. Dining here is a celebration for the senses and France's best wine-waiter takes care of the wines. Also a hotel.

Clos Saint-Vincent
☎ 89.73.67.65
Situated high above Ribeauvillé in the midst of vineyards. The view is exceptionally beautiful. The cooking is also very good here; the weekday lunch menu costs around FF 150 and offers good value for your money. It is also a luxurious hotel (prices starting at FF 600).

La Flammerie
☎ 89.73.61.08
Simple eating-house along the Grand'Rue. Excellent, generous *baekeoffe*, tasty *tarte flambée*.

grape varieties.

Robert Faller The very dark, brown office and shop of Jean-Baptiste Faller is situated in the Grand'Rue. Specialities of the wine estate are the Riesling Giesberg and Gewurztraminer Kirchberg.

Henri Fuchs Small winegrower with very creditable wines, such as Pinot Blanc and Tokay Pinot Gris.

Kientzler This is one of the top wine estates of the Alsace. André Kientzler is able to create a number of extraordinary wines. To name a few: Auxerrois K, Muscat Kirchberg, Riesling Geisberg, Riesling Osterberg. A charming Chasselas is also made from the Osterberg.

Zum Pfifferhüs
✆ 89.73.62.28
An almost legendary winstub with strictly regional dishes.

Winstub with a good reputation.

Les Vosges
✆ 89.73.61.39
The kitchen here has developed into one of the best in the area, thanks to well thought-out creations. Comfortable interior, very attentive service. Menus from FF 160 (lunch during the week).

The Louis Sipp house.

The place de la Sinn.

The city hall is a solid building dating from the 18th century. It is worth entering the high, wooden doors, because inside the building a small, civic museum has been established. Across from the *hôtel de ville* stands a 14th century, grey, Augustinian, monastery church with a multi-coloured roof. Slightly further, the flat-topped Butcher's tower (13th century) rises. Formerly, Ribeauvillé consisted of three fortified districts; towers separated the upper town from the centre. Further along the Grand'Rue is a shop with tempting items such as *foie gras*, before one arrives at the place de la Sinn. This has a fountain with a large, 19th century statue and various half- timbered houses near to it. The parish church of Saint-Grégoire-le-Grand stands nearby. Its construction took almost two centuries (starting in the 13th century); the portal carries a sculpted tympanum. The Grand'Rue finishes at the triangular place de la République, where a

Jean Sipp Delicious wines of all qualities: Edelzwicker, Riesling Kirchberg de Ribeauvillé, Tokay Pinot Gris, etc.
Louis Sipp Correct wines, in part from their own land. Among the specialities of this wine merchant are the Pinot Blanc, Riesling Kirchberg de Ribeauvillé and the Gewurztraminer Osterberg.

Trimbach Wines of a high average quality. The Riesling Clos Ste. Hune is the absolute top of its type, while the Riesling Cuvée Frédéric Emile and the Gewurztraminer Cuvée des Seigneurs de Ribeaupierre are also magnificent wines. The less spectacular (and less costly) wines are also of a high standard, such as

Renaissance fountain is situated.
Some small industries are established in Ribeauvillé, among others, printed fabrics (to be bought in various shops). Moreover, Carola mineral water is bottled here, in a complex which also has a swimming pool and a restaurant. The emphasis, though, is still placed on wine,

Trimbach's small tower.

thanks to a large cooperative, a number of wine taverns and private *vignerons.*
Three of Ribeauvillé's vineyards belong to the category of grand cru: Geisberg, Kirchberg and Osterberg. In general, they produce mainly Riesling, with Gewurztraminer in second place.

TOURIST TIPS
• At the beginning of June the Fête du Kugelhopf takes place. It is a time to eat one's fill of this fruit-cake – a true Alsatian delicacy. Of course, there is also wine and music.
• In the park, near the entrance to Ribeauvillé, stands a statue of a minstrel.
• By means of the rue du 3 Décembre, one drives out of the centre back onto the wine route. Along this street, a large pottery is situated. Note the view across the city centre.

This evening a bäckeoffa stew is being served.

the Sylvaner Sélection, the Pinot Blanc fermented in wood, the Muscat, the Tokay Pinot Gris and the Gewurztraminer (all preferably in the categories Réserve Personnelle or Réserve).

RELATED TO WINE
• Ribeauvillé has its own wine exchange,

which is always held during the second half of July.
• In the city, orange signposts point the way to wine producers.
• Jean-Paul Metté is one of the best distillers of the Alsace. He distils many *eaux-de-vie,* including a sublime framboise.

A winegrower's house.

Tourist Tips
- If driving, starting on the route du vin, to Hunawihr, the Centre de Réintroduction de Cigognes lies to the left of the approach road. This works towards the improvement of conditions for storks in Alsace. It may be visited. They are also setting up a conservatory for live butterflies.
- The fortified church is attended by Catholics as well as by Protestants.
- The local city hall dates from 1517.

Hunawihr

One of the most striking sights to see in Alsace is a fortified church standing on a hill above Hunawihr. This protected monument and its churchyard are surrounded by a thick rampart with six half-rounded bastions. The building dates mostly from the 14th and 15th centuries. The choir is Gothic and dates from 1524. The church also contains 14 (somewhat faded) frescos with representations from the life of Saint Nicolas. Hunawihr's connection with winegrowing is symbolized by the hands of the tower clock, which are decorated with bunches of grapes. The village received its name from Huna, who lived in the 7th century. She did much charity work and washed the clothes of the sick in a fountain. This stands at the foot of the church hill. Legend has it that the water in the fountain once changed into wine after a poor wine harvest.

A unique fortified church is situated above Hunawihr.

Recommended Producers
Cooperative Stars are the Crémant Calixite II, Muscat, Tokay Pinot Gris, the Rieslings Muehlforst and Rosacker and the Gewurztraminers Windsbuhl and Rosacker.
Jean-Luc Mader Fine Rieslings.
Frédéric Mallo & Fils Soft, distinguished wines, such as Muscat, Tokay Pinot Gris, Riesling Rosacker, Gewurztraminer Rosacker, Gewurztraminer Mandelberg.

Related to Wine
- Hunawihr has its own grand cru, the Rosacker.
- The Riesling Clos Ste. Hune of Trimbach is famous.

ZELLENBERG

The position of Zellenberg is unique, because this small, narrow village is built on the top of a 120 metre high hill. The counts of Ribeaupierre had a beautiful castle there but after the French Revolution this was sold stone by stone. There now remain only two towers. One of these stands next to the Baroque church of Saint-Ulrich (1760) and carries a stork's nest.

Zellenberg consists of not much more than three streets which run parallel. The most easterly runs to Ostheim in the plain. Via both of the others, one can walk around the village centre. There are various buildings dating from the 16th and 17th centuries.

The village takes its name from the word cella, or cell, because in the 9th century the hill was deforested by monks who afterwards built a small monastic cell.

Zellenberg is situated on top of a 120 metre high hill.

HOTELS
Au Riesling
℮ 89.47.85.85
Rather modern hotel with a tapered roof. A number of the 36 rooms offer a view across the Rhine plain. Prices start at around FF 250. It is owned by a winegrowing family and is also a restaurant.

Le Schlossberg
℮ 89.47.93.85
This is the only hotel in the old centre. Four of the seven rooms have a terrace and offer a view across Riquewihr. They cost around FF 500. Rooms on street level are around FF 350. Across from the hotel is a restaurant with a cosy bar. The speciality is *baekeoffe.* Menus begin at about FF 200. Large wine list.

RESTAURANT
Maximilien
℮ 89.47.99.69
Pink building with neon sign. Contemporary quality cuisine in a modern interior. Dinner menus begin at approximately FF 200.

RECOMMENDED PRODUCERS
J.Becker Wine merchant. The Sylvaner F, Muscat, Muscat Froehn, Tokay Pinot Gris and Pinot Gris Rimeltsberg, Riesling Réserve and Hagenschlauf, Gewurztraminer and Gewurztraminer Froehn Pinot Noir.
Aphonse Fux Muscat, Tokay Pinot Gris, a Pinot Noir matured in wooden vats.

Jean Huttard Riesling Lerchenberg, Muscat Réserve, Gewurztraminer Réserve.
Edmond Rentz Excellent Tokay Pinot Gris.
Marcel Rentz Pinot Blanc.

RELATED TO WINE
• The Froehn is a grand cru.

The slightly sloping main street of Riquewihr.

RIQUEWIHR

'Whoever has not seen Riquewihr, has not seen Alsace', according to an old saying, because as far as beauty, atmosphere and character are concerned, this village, surrounded by vineyards, is the epitome of what Alsace has to offer. Riquewihr is like a large museum, of which the collection consists of dozens of 16th and 17th century buildings, old wells and fountains, skilful woodcarving, intimate courtyards with galleries, marvellous bay windows and portals, worked stone tablets, weather-stained statues, colourful signboards, cellars and churches, a local castle, fortified towers, double ramparts and the multi-

HOTELS

La Couronne
© 89.49.03.03
Modern comfort in an old building. It stands in the centre of Riquewihr (rue de la Couronne). The 40 rooms have prices starting just under FF 300.

Le Riquewihr
© 89.47.83.13
Situated just outside the village, in the midst of vineyards. Nice, rustically decorated rooms, almost 50 in number. Sauna. Prices start at around FF 225.

RECOMMENDED PRODUCERS
Jean-Jacques Baumann & Fils Capable producer. Riesling Schoenenbourg, Riesling Birgelé, Tokay Pinot Gris Kobelsberg, Gewurztraminer, Gewurztraminer Sporen: each one a wine of high quality. The family Baumann has taken over vineyards from producer René Schmidt.

Raymond Berschy In any case taste the Pinot Blanc, Muscat and Riesling here.
Ernest Bronner An almost confidential harvest of Muscat, Riesling Schoenenbourg and diverse types of Gewurztraminer.
Dopff & Irion Wines of a correct quality. A few of the better ones are the Muscat

coloured splendour of flowers. Riquewihr, in short, is a delight for the eye. Unfortunately, there is the drawback that the village attracts an enormous number of visitors. On summer weekends the whole length of the outer rampart is full of parked cars (driving by non-inhabitants is forbidden in Riquewihr), while at the eastern gateway one coach after another pours out its passengers. At such times, the village contains around 20,000 people, more than five times the number of inhabitants. It is therefore unwise to visit Riquewihr on a weekend. Go during the week, and then preferably in the morning. As a result of tourism, the village has a flourishing trade: numerous shops sell souvenirs and regional products, including wine. Various local producers have shops in Riquewihr (with or without a tasting room). A few even run a winstub. Although, graves have been found near Rique-

Le Schoenenbourg
© 89.49.01.11
This hotel has existed since 1975,and in 1991 received a new wing. It is situated at the foot of the vineyard of the same name, next to *Auberge du Schoenenbourg* (the same owners). Tastefully designed rooms (45), with all conveniences. Prices from FF 300 to about FF 500 (new wing).

RESTAURANTS

Au Petit Gourmet
© 89.47.98.77
Located in the same street as Hugel. The décor is completely Alsatian. The cuisine offers, apart from the well-known regional specialities, more surprising fare. Menus from FF 200.

Le Sarment d'Or
© 89.47.92.85
In the vaulted, tastefully decorated dining room, one can enjoy regional specialities prepared with care and good wines. The three course menu (approximately FF 100), above all, gives good value for your money.

↑ *The Dolder, in which a small museum is situated.*
← *Riquewihr seen from the Schoenenbourg vineyard.*

Les Amandiers and Muscat Schoenenbourg, Gewurztraminer Les Sorcières and Sporen, and Riesling Les Murailles.
Dopff au Moulin The wine merchant Dopff au Moulin has a cellar complex on the east side of Riquewihr and is one of the most important producers of Alsace. The Crémant brands include Cuvée Julien,

Wild Brut and Blanc de Noirs. Still wines of class are, among others, Muscat Réserve, Tokay Pinot Gris Réserve, Riesling Schoenenbourg, Gewurztraminer Sporen, Gewurztraminer Brand. Château du Moulin is a wine made from three varieties with a soft, fresh taste and the fruit of the muscat.

Auberge du Schoe-nenbourg

✆ 89.47.92.28

The business has developed into one of the best in the region. The interior is light and exceptionally stylish. The dining room, which is furnished with a lot of glass, is partially surrounded by a terrace. A very refined cuisine, in which surprising tastes are subtly and agreeably combined. Usually there are two menus under FF 200. Excellent wine selection, friendly service.

Le Tire-Bouchon

✆ 89.47.91.61

This winstub, situated on the main street, is a good place for *choucroute* and *baeckeoffe*. Property of the house of Preiss-Zimmer.

wihr dating from the Merovingian period (5th up to and including 8th centuries) little is known about the origins of the village. In the 14th century it was called Reichenweier, or 'rich village'. Even then the inhabitants earned good money through wine.

In 1291, the city received permission to build city ramparts. The earliest monuments also date from that year, such as the northern wall and the Dolder, a 25 metre high tower near the western gateway. Nowadays, a small archeological museum is located in it, with among things, a collection of weapons, utensils and painted roofing tiles.

In the 16th century Riquewihr experienced its heyday. It had an active winegrowers association, which protected the quality of the wines, and at that time a second, lower city rampart was built around the first. During that century the first manor houses of well-to-do citizens arose, as well as the castle of the Princes of Württemberg-Montbéliard. This stands slightly to the left of the eastern entrance, which forms the best starting point for a walk through Riquewihr. One enters the village here by means of the gateway under the city hall, a solid-looking building dating from the 19th century. Whereas part of the castle belongs to the wine-house Dopff & Irion, the other wing accommodates a very interesting postal museum. Here, a regional history of 2000 years of post service and telecommunica-

The city hall.

Hugel & Fils It is very likely that the emergence of wines with the titles *vendange tardive* and *sélection des grains nobles* is largely thanks to the commercial successes made by Hugel long before most other producers made these types of wine. The *vendanges tardives*, in particular, still comprise a strong division of the

range: Gewurztraminer Tokay Pinot and Riesling. Of the ordinary dry wines, the following, among others, are worth seeking: Edelzwicker (various brands), Pinot Blanc Cuvée les Amours, Riesling Tradition, Réserve and Cuvée Jubilee, Tokay Pinot Gris Cuvée Jubilee, many versions of Gewurztraminer, wood-matured Pinot

tions has been exhibited. Stamp collectors will really enjoy themselves here.

Back on the main street – which divides Riquewihr from the *hôtel de ville* to the Dolder – you can take pleasure in one marvellous building after another. For instance, there is a magnificent half-timbered house with a tapered roof, the Maison Trim, dating from 1606. Likewise, on the main street, there is also the Maison au Nid de Cigognes, dating from 1535, which is named after its stork's nest. Note the inner courtyard with its balcony, signboard (with stork), 17th century well and large press dating from 1817.

A little further, on the second corner on the left, is the wine-cellar of Hugel & Fils. This family has made wine since 1639. The building on the corner on the right has a depiction of a cooper on its wooden gable. The side street alongside it runs to the church (1846). The two adjacent buildings were formerly also churches but, since the 16th century, have been houses. None the less, the street is still called rue des Trois Eglises. At number 42, on the main street, the signboard (1928) – much photographed – of the

Various wine taverns have their own shops.

Noir and the blended wine Sporen (as long as this remains legally in existence in accordance with the grand cru regulation).

Roger Jung Independent winegrower with a series of fine wines. Riesling, Riesling Schoenenbourg, Riesling Sporen, Tokay Pinot Gris Rosenbourg, Gewurztra-

miner Sporen.

Philippe Leisibach Absolutely delicious Muscat, very aromatic.

Mittnacht-Klack Family wine estate which has made wine for generations; the grapevines stand in five towns. Muscat, Tokay Pinot Gris, Rieslings (generic, Saint-Ulrich, Muehlforst, Rosacker,

- Near the Château de Riquewihr (postal museum) is a small open-air museum with, among other exhibits, stone sculptures and an altar dating from 1790.
- In the cellars of Hugel stands a large vat dating from 1715, with wood carving.
- In summer, on Friday evenings, a son et lumière spectacle takes place (sometimes also on Wednesday evenings).

A statue above a fountain.

famous Alsatian painter/draughtsman Hansi, indicates that the Preiss-Henny wine-house has its headquarters here. Earlier, the 17th century building served as an inn. A passageway runs to the Cour de Vignerons, where the sessions of the wine-growers association took place.

Just before the Dolder, at the place de la Sinn, there is a fountain dating from 1560. To the right of it runs the rue des Juifs to the Thieves Towers. Visitors can shudder looking at the prison cell, torture chamber, strappado and vanishing pit. The best walk back is through the rue du Cerf and other narrow streets on the south side of the main street: many beautiful houses stand there, most of which are in perfect condition.

The impressive wine slope, which rises on the northern side of Riquewihr, is the grand cru Schoenenbourg, the home of, above all, great Rieslings. To the southeast of the village lies the Sporen, likewise a grand cru. Gewurztraminer and Tokay Pinot Gris are its most famous wines.

Hansi's sign.

Schoenenbourg) and Gewurztraminer (amongst others, Rosacker).
Preiss-Zimmer Small wine merchant which makes truly dry wines. It sells about 10 per cent of its volume in Riquewihr itself (shop and winstub *Le Tire-Bouchon*. Top wines are the Rieslings Réserve Personnelle, Brand, Schoenenbourg and

Sporen, and the Riesling and Gewurztraminer Cuvée de Beaumont. Pleasant Sylvaner. Property of the cooperative of Turckheim.

BEBLENHEIM

Driving in a southerly
direction from Rique-
wihr, you come first
to a large 'camping
intercommunal',

The Gothic Bawla-fountain (right).

which is centrally lo-
cated in regard to various towns. The turn-off to
Beblenheim then follows very quickly. By turning
immediately left, one comes onto the road that
leads to the best vineyards in Beblenheim, the
grand cru Sonnenglanz. At the end of the road –
which passes, among others, the house of winegrower Jean-Paul Hartweg – a fine and unusual

The local wine cooperative.

view across
Zellenberg
can be en-
joyed. The
village street
winds past
half-tim-
bered houses
and the
Gothic
Bawla foun-

tain (15th century). A little further on is the wine
cooperative. The rue Jean Macé – named after the
villager who founded the first village library –
runs not only to the wine house Bott-Geyl, but
also to a wine vat with woodcarving (near la
Grange Beranger).

RESTAURANT
Le Bouc Bleu
☏ 89.47.88.21
Small restaurant (35
seats) with a boldly
coloured façade. Rural
and at the same time in-
ventive cuisine. Menus
from about FF 120.

TOURIST TIP
• Beblenheim is the
birthplace of Christian
Oberlin, who is con-
sidered to be one of
the pioneers of Alsa-
tian winegrowing. At
the end of the last
century he collected
every possible grape
variety. He also found-
ed the Institute Viti-
cole of Colmar.

Artistic wood carving.

RECOMMENDED PRODUCERS
Bott-Gey Small wine merchant, which
obtains practically all of its wines from its
own land. Pinot Blanc, Riesling Mandelberg, a few Sonnenglanz wines (varying
quality). A wine cellar full of atmosphere
with an old winepress and large casks.
Cooperative Reasonably priced Alsatians of decent quality, for example, the
Pinot Blanc, but also produces high-class
wines such as the Gewurztraminer Sonnenglanz and a good Crémant.
Jean-Paul Hartweg Lives next to the
Sonnenglanz and produces a Tokay Pinot
Gris and Gewurztraminer from this land
as his best wines.

MITTELWIHR

While Beblenheim and Riquewihr, to all intents
and purposes, remained undamaged, Mittelwihr
was totally destroyed in the Second World War.
Only a few sections of the church remained,
among them the 15th century clock tower. The

The clock tower.

'Wall of the Martyrs'
Flowers', on the main
street, also escaped
destruction. The wall
received its name be-
cause, during the Sec-
ond World War, the
inhabitants decorated
it thrice with blue
convolvulus, white
petunias and red ge-
raniums – the colours
of the *tricolore* – and
the Gestapo cut them
down three times. In
1944, the castle of
Mittelwihr was totally lost; it continues to exist
only in old engravings.

On the west side of the village are vineyards
which are protected by hills and mountains on
three sides. Because of this there is an extremely
mild microclimate, which is good for the grapes –
above all in the grand cru Mandelberg. Mittelwihr seems to be the only village in Alsace where
almonds grow; the nuts are used in the local delicacy *manteltarte*.

RECOMMENDED PRODUCERS
Jean Greiner A generous Gewurztrami-
ner Mandelberg.
Edgar Schaller & Fils His Crémant and
Muscat are delicious. Various Rieslings.
Philippe Scheidecker Beautiful Mus-
cat and fine Rieslings.
J.Siegler Père & Fils A Tokay Pinot Gris

which is usually successful.
Specht A complement for the Muscat, Tokay Pinot Gris and Riesling Mandelberg.
Bernard Wurtz Riesling Mandelberg and
an often impressive Tokay Pinot Gris.
Jean-Jacques Ziegler-Mauler Striking
wines. Tokay Pinot Gris, Riesling Cuvée de
la Toussaint, Gewurztraminer.

The Marckrain can be tested.

BENNWIHR

Just like Mittelwihr, which it borders, Bennwihr was entirely destroyed in December 1944. By a touch of fate, only the monument to the victims of the First World War was spared. The building that attracts most attention is the modern church of Saint-Pierre. From outside it gives a cool, austere impression but inside one is almost overwhelmed by the warm colours of the stained glass windows, which give the interior a particular touch of distinction. The building was finished in 1960.
For the rest, Bennwihr is not much more than a long street with a few short sidestreets. The vicissitudes of the war destroyed almost all the grapevines, so the winegrowers began to restore them collectively via a wine cooperative. This has grown into one of the largest in Alsace. The firm is strongly focused on tourists, who arrive in droves in coaches.

RESTAURANT
Relais Hansi
✆ 89.47.80.31
This is the cooperative's restaurant, and they naturally serve their own wines. It has space for about 300 guests. Strictly regional cuisine, mostly good standard and reasonable prices. In the restaurant there is a press dating from 1948.

The cooperative's restaurant.

The wine festival in the middle of August.

RECOMMENDED PRODUCER
Cooperative Brings wines onto the market for mass distribution; their quality and price are based upon this. Among the most attractive types are the Crémant, Pinot Noir (vat matured and Gewurztraminer vendange tardive.

RELATED TO WINE
- The Marckrain grand cru lies within the towns of Bennwihr and Sigolsheim. In general, the wines lack true distinction, although the Gewurztraminer can sometimes taste delicious.
- Bennwihr celebrates its Fête du Vin in the middle of August.

Sigolsheim once won a prize as the village with the most beautiful roofs.

RESTAURANT
Au Bon Coin
✆ 89.78.22.33
Simple eating house on the church square. Fish specialities such as baked carp fillets, but also a *salade gourmande* with *foie gras maison* and *brioche de foie gras maison*.

SIGOLSHEIM

It is not only by reading the signs and wine signposts that one realizes Sigolsheim is a wine village, one also smells it – at least during harvest time. Then the whole village gives off the scent of wine. Present-day Sigolsheim – where the roofs once won an award – is peacefully sited at the foot of one of the largest grands crus in Alsace, the Mambourg. It is difficult to imagine that this place was a bloody theatre of war in 1944. The Allies and Germans fought fiercely over it. The Couvent des Capucins, which lies next to the Mambourg, was taken and retaken at least 15 times. A constant reminder of this horrible

RECOMMENDED PRODUCERS
Cooperative A very large and very well equipped firm, which was founded in 1946. It makes a large range of varied wines. A few of the most successful are the Gewurztraminer Mambourg, Tokay Pinot Gris and Muscat. More standard wines are also found.

Ringenbach-Moser A small wine house which has, as its specialities, Gewurztraminer and Tokay Pinot Gris. Above all, those from the Mambourg are delicious.
Pierre Schillé & Fils Solid working family wine estate with land in various towns. Pinot Blanc, Gewurztraminer (also from the Mambourg).

period is given by the National Military Cemetery which is on top of the Mambourg; 1590 soldiers of the First French army found their final resting place there.

TOURIST TIP
• From the road to the Military Cemetary, one has a view across the wide surrounding landscape.

Tympanum above the vestibule.

After the wine cellars had been repaired, Sigolsheim was rebuilt with care. The church of Saint-Pierre-et-Saint-Paul, Romanesque in orgin, was also restored. Above the portal is a tympanum, on which a kneeling winegrower is seen offering Saint Paul a vat of wine. Saint Peter, on the other hand, receives a pouch of money. Under the tympanum, curious animals are depicted. The interior of the church is rather sober.

Sigolsheim can boast a very long history of winemaking. The village already existed around 700 and the first mention of vineyards dates from 783. The microclimate could be a reason for this: local winegrowers say that the Mambourg is one of the warmest parts of the region, because the snow often melts here first.

Situated at the foot of wine hills.

Pierre Sparr The Sparr family has produced wine for a good three centuries, in part from substantial private land. The average quality of the best wines rose considerably in the 1980s. Examples are the Pinot Blanc, Riesling SPS, Riesling Mambourg, Riesling Schlossberg, Tokay Pinot Gris (various *cuvées*), Gewurztraminer Brand, Gewurztraminer Mambourg and the Crémant.

RELATED TO WINE
• The Mambourg lies entirely within Sigolsheim. Aside from this the village owns parts of the grands crus of Marckrain and Schlossberg.

The village gateway with its Lalli.

KIENTZHEIM

Coming from the direction of Sigolsheim or Ammerschwihr a visitor to Kientzheim is welcomed by the Lalli, a monstrous face that sticks its tongue out from high up in the city gate. The head was intended not only to alarm attackers, but also to help to drive them away, because the throat is also a loophole.

To the right of the gate one can begin a walk of about 20 minutes over the ramparts. They were constructed on the orders of Count Jean de Lupfen and date from the 15th century.

To the left of the gate stands the Château de Kientzheim. It is the creation of administrator and imperial general Lazare de Schwendi (1522-1583), who apparently brought the pinot gris grape out of Hungary after his campaign against the Turks. The castle rose up upon the foundations of an older bulwark; thus it has a cellar dating from the 13th century. In a dilapidated state after the Second World War, it became the property of the Confrérie Saint-Etienne. This wine fraternity has renovated the whole construction and uses it for its events. What's more, the Musée du Vignoble et des Vins d'Alsace is housed in the castle. This contains a comprehensive collection of wine-related objects

HOTEL
Hostellerie de l'Abbaye d'Alspach
℡ 89.47.16.00
About 30 rather compact, quite modern rooms around the courtyard of a former abbey. It is situated just off the main street. Prices from around FF 250 to around FF 350. Also a restaurant.

RECOMMENDED PRODUCERS
André Blanck & Fils Has cellars just behind the Château de Kientzheim. Riesling Schlossberg, Gewurztraminer.
Blanck/Domaine des Comtes de Lupfen Very dynamic wine family. The grapes are vinified by variety and soil type, with a long series of exemplary wines as a result. Among them are Edelzwicker (as Cuvée des Comtes de Lupfen), Pinot d'Alsace, Klevner Réserve, Sylvaner Réserve, Muscat, Tokay Pinot Gris (-Réserve Spéciale, Patergarten, Altenbourg), Riesling (Altenbourg, Furstentum, Schlossberg), Gewurztraminer (Altenbourg), Pinot Noir.

and documents, which are attractively exhibited and demonstrate perfectly the turbulent and long history of Alsatian viniculture. Past the castle, at a bend in the village street, stands a fountain with the names of grape varieties on its sides. In the village church the gravestones of Schwendi and

One side of the fountain.

his son, a Gothic choir and a Baroque altar can be found. The pilgrimage chapel of Notre-Dame (rebuilt after the war) has a unique collection of *ex votos*. A ruined tank near the western village gateway is a reminder of the ravages of war – which, happily, did not strike Kientzheim very hard.

Surrounded by grapevines.

Cooperative In the 1980s the *cave coopérative* invested heavily in new equipment which has been very beneficial for the quality of the wines. This shows in, among others, the Sylvaner, Pinot Blanc, Tokay Pinot Gris, Muscat, Riesling Schlossberg, Gewurztraminer Kaefferkopf, Gewurztraminer Furstentum and Crémant.

RESTAURANT
Château du Reichenstein
✆ 89.47.15.88
This castle stands near the western village gateway. It dates from the 15th century and was restored between 1955 and 1956. One eats in the former, vaulted hunting hall. The menu offers classic regional, as well as more sophisticated dishes and starts at about FF 150.

TOURIST TIP
• Take the road, near the fountain with the bunches of grapes, which runs out of the village and rises up to the Schlossberg. From this grand cru one has a view across Kientzheim and the neighbouring villages.

RELATED TO WINE
• In the last weekend of July, a festival of wine and folklore takes place. Historic procession and free wine from the fountain.
• Parts of two grands crus lie within the area, the Schlossberg (Alsace's first) and Furstentum.

KAYSERSBERG

The former Mons Caesaris or Mountain of Caesar is strategically situated in the Weiss valley, one of the most important routes between France and the Rhine valley. In 1227 it is mentioned for the first time as Kaysersberg. This occurred when the village and the Middle Age castle lying above it were sold to Emperor Frederick II. In the same year he fortified Kaysersberg with ramparts. The many, fine patrician houses and other buildings, dating from the 15th, 16th and 17th centuries, prove that the area knew a long period of prosperity.

HOTELS
A l'Arbre Vert
℗ 89.47.11.51
Comprises about 20 rooms on the large square close to the Schweitzer house. Rural comfort, prices starting at around FF 250. The restaurant (with a terrace in front) is exceptionally cosy – and one eats well. Menus commence at around FF 120. In season the fresh asparagus here tastes delicious, and the *truite au Crémant d'Alsace* is

↑ *The castle, seen from between two half-timbered houses; to the left is an old bath house.*
← *Kaysersberg's church has a remarkable clock tower.*

RECOMMENDED PRODUCERS
Faller/Domaine Weinbach Along the road between Kientzheim and Kaysersberg lies the walled Clos des Capucins. This is the property of Colette Faller and her family, who run the Domaine Weinbach. This is by far the largest wine estate of Kaysersbach. The quality of the

wines is very high (like the prices). Here, very pure, always excellent wines are made, full of seductive charms. To name but a few: Sylvaner, Pinot Blanc, Muscat, the Rieslings Réserve Personnelle, Cuvée Théo, Schlossberg and Cuvée de la Sainte-Catherine, the Tokay Pinot Gris Cuvée de la Sainte-Catherine and the Ge-

worth trying. Across from the *A l'Arbre Vert* lies *La Belle Promenade*, a somewhat modern and more luxurious annexe with 30 rooms.

The museum and a caveau.

Hôtel des Remparts
℗ 89.47.12.12
Modern, peacefully situated hotel (`at the foot of the grapevine and the woods') which was fully restored a few years ago. Around 30 rooms. Average price FF 350.

A good starting point for a visit is the eastern entrance of the main street (from the direction of Kientzheim). The rue du Général de Gaulle, which alternates between being narrow and wide, has fine half-timbered houses and residences in Renaissance style on both sides. Here one will also find many good shops for souvenirs, ceramics, regional delicacies, wines and distillates.

After a few dozen metres, you will find the small church square to your right, and also the city hall, a building dating from 1521 with a beautiful façade and an inner courtyard with a wooden balcony. Dating from the same year is the fountain on the square, with a statue of Emperor Constantine, the first Christian emperor, on it. Above its 13th century portal, the church contains a marvellous tympanum which not only shows the crowning of the Virgin Mary by two Archangels, but also the sculptor. Inside there are many things to admire, such as an enormous Crucifixion group and a sublime, 16th century triptych behind the main altar. Near the church is sited a two-storeyed chapel with a 15th century fresco and a small Military Cemetery for those who fell in 1944. A little further along the main street is the municipal museum, which is certainly worth a visit.

wurztraminer Cuvée Laurence.
Salzmann Thomann Serious winegrowing family with, among others, an attractive Riesling and Gewurztraminer Schlossberg.

RELATED TO WINE
• Part of the grand cru Schlossberg falls within the municipality of Kaysersberg.

A wine and distillate store.

One of the most famous exhibits is a rare statue of a Holy Virgin, which can be opened (14th century).

Where the main street makes a right-angled turn to the left, there is a half-timbered house with an open gallery in its façade. Straight on to the right stands a large building which formerly served as a bath house. Between the two buildings a path runs to the castle ruin. This has a sturdy moat tower which offers a view across the oldest section of Kaysersberg.

Next to the bath house, a 16th century fortified bridge crosses the Weiss which flows fast here. From the bridge there is a nice view of old houses

RESTAURANTS

Au Lion d'Or
✆ 89.47.11.16
A restaurant in the main street which is almost always busy. *Choucroute*, game when in season: stuffed quail with *foie gras*. The cuisine in this centuries-old building is rural and regional. Menus from around FF 100.

Chambard
✆ 89.47.10.17
Situated by the eastern entrance to the village. In the spacious rooms (capacity 150 guests) of this stylishly furnished restaurant one will enjoy a very pleasant stay. The cuisine is refined, surprising and tasty, based on superior ingredients, while the service is very attentive. Menus start at around

From the fortified bridge across the Weiss.

FF 250. Large selection of wines. Chambard also has 20 very comfortable hotel rooms (prices from FF 500).

TOURIST TIPS
- On the well, which stands on the inner courtyard of number 54 on the main street, one can read a humorous text. It recommends leaving the water in the well and, instead, drinking a subtle wine when seated, for a meal.
- In Lapoutroie, a few kilometres into the Vosges, an *eau-de-vie* museum can be found (at the distillers).
- Around the village four fortified towers from the 15th century still stand.

against the backdrop of the Vosges. Not far past the bridge is the house where Albert Schweitzer was born in 1875. The building contains a museum which gives an overview of the life of the theologian, philosopher, musician, doctor, author and benefactor. The house is easily recognized by the pointed tower on its gabled roof.

After passing the fortified bridge, one can also turn right to the Oberhof Chapel. This was built in 1391 and contains a 15th century statue of Christ with a bunch of grapes. By turning immediately left when across the bridge, one comes to the rue des Poitiers, with old tanners' houses. Another small bridge across the Weiss then leads one back to the village centre.

The imposing dwelling of the Domaine Weinbach.

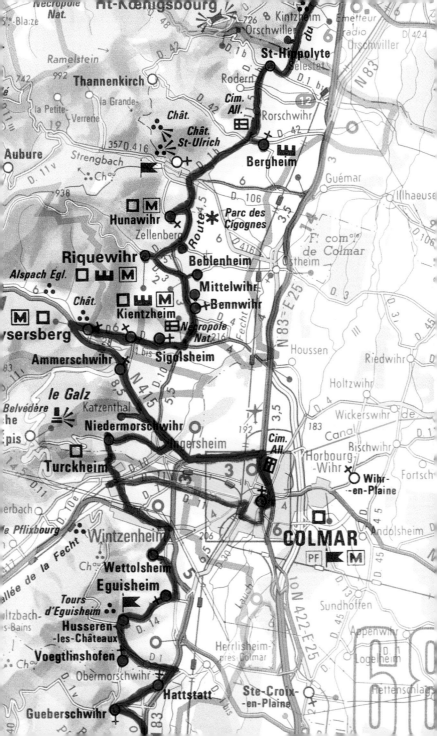

AMMERSCHWIHR

The busy N 415, which connects Saint-Dié with Colmar (via Kaysersberg), runs directly through Ammerschwihr, the largest wine municipality in Alsace. On the eastern side of the *route nationale* lies a rather modern and constantly cultivated district with, behind it, flat vineyards. On the western side one finds the old village centre, beside which the hill of the famous Kaefferkopf vineyard rises up. The old, completely 16th cen-

A view of the village from the Kaefferkopf.

tury Ammerschwihr – where Queen Wilhelmina of the Netherlands used to paint – was largely destroyed in 1944. Luckily, the village was rebuilt

RECOMMENDED PRODUCERS
Adam Pinot Blanc, Muscat, Tokay Pinot Gris Cuvée Jean-Baptiste, Rieslings of Kaefferkopf and Letzenberg, Gewurztraminer Kaefferkopf, Pinot Noir and others.
Claude Dietrich Pinot Blanc, Tokay Pinot Gris, Riesling Schlossberg, Gewurztraminers of Altenbourg and Vogelgarten.

Henri Ehrhart Edelzwicker, Pinot Blanc, Riesling, Gewurztraminer Kaefferkopf.
Jérôme Geschickt & Fils Sylvaner, Rieslings, Gewurztraminer Kaefferkopf, Pinot Noir.
Henri et Joseph Heitzmann Riesling, Gewurztraminer Kaefferkopf and others.
Roger Klein Gewurztraminer of the Clos

with much taste and care, as one will clearly see in a half hour walk. At the traffic lights along the N 415 is a large parking area. Across from it stands the round Tour des Fripons (Rogue tower). In this 16th century monument a tasting room has been established.

From the tower, the Grand'Rue leads into the village. Directly to the left one finds the restaurant *Aux Armes de France*, with the Kuehn wine tavern next to it. Slightly further along, the main street leads to the ruins of the former town hall (left, dating from 1522), which has been declared a monument. In front of the present *hôtel de ville* (just to the right) lies a square containing the Fontaine de l'Homme Sauvage, which dates from the 16th century.

One may walk on further between the attractive residences. The street becomes narrower, is cobbled and runs gently uphill. At the end stands the proud Porte-Haute, a fortified, 13th century tower with a sundial and a stork's nest. By turning left, one comes to the Tour des Bourgeois (16th century, with a tasting room). The Saint-Martin church is not far away, dating from the 16th century, with high pillars, an enormous Cruxifixion from 1606 and other religious works of art. In mid-August Ammerschwihr celebrates the festival of the Kaefferkopf.

RESTAURANT
Aux Armes de France
✆ 89.47.10.12
This is one of the most renowned names in Alsace. The two spacious dining rooms, situated on the first floor, with their blue/beige chairs and curtains, are very comfortable. The service is attentive and quiet, the wine list is gigantic and the food delicious, with variations on classic themes. In any case, taste the *foie gras d'oie* and the *sorbet au Marc de Gewurztraminer*. The Riesling, served by the carafe, has an astounding quality and a low price. Menus start at around FF 350 (less expensive lunch menu during the week). There are 10 hotel rooms available.

TOURIST TIPS
• Near Ammerschwihr there is an 18-hole golf course.
• In the Kaefferkopf the remains of Château Meywihr are to be found (futher along from the rue du Cerf).
• A lovely road to Katzenthal runs through Kaefferkopf.

Meywihr (lies within the Kaefferkopf).
Kuehn Pinot Blanc, Gewurztraminer Cuvée Saint-Hubert and Riesling.
Domaine Martin Schaetzel Sylvaner, Pinot Blanc, Auxerrois, Tokay Pinot Gris, Riesling, Gewurztraminer, Pinot Noir.
Domaine François Schiélé The speciality of Charles Schiélé is Riesling.

Maurice Schoech Edelzwicker, Tokay Pinot Gris, Riesling and Gewurztraminer Kaefferkopf. A lot of class.
Sick-Dreyer Klevner, Tokay Pinot Gris, Riesling and Gewurztraminer Kaefferkopf.

RELATED TO WINE
• Alsatian wine exchange (April).

KATZENTHAL

Two buildings determine the silhouette of Katzenthal, a small village about one kilometre from the
N 415: a slim, white church tower and the ruins of
Château Wineck. The tower, like most of the
houses, dates from after 1944, because by that time
Katzenthal had been, for the larger part, destroyed. The castle dates from the 11th and 12th centuries and was already dilapidated by the 16th century. However, since 1971 it has been slowly under-
going restoration
by volunteers.

All the roads to
Katzenthal are
fringed by grape-
vines, because the
village lies in the
midst of undulat-
ing wine hills.
Around the castle
the best local Ries-
lings are produced
from the Wineck-

Entering the village from the N 415.

Schlossberg grand
cru. Its slopes are steep; the castle appears to be
overwhelmed by vines. The centre of Katzenthal
takes the form of a reclining groove: it is, for the
most part, surrounded, on both sides and at the
highest point, by streets without pavements,
which converge by the fountain. The houses have
a very cared-for look and in the village there is a
general air of benevolent peace.

RECOMMENDED PRODUCERS
Jean-Marc Bernhard Creditable wines,
among them a Muscat.
Jean-Paul Ecklé Authoritative wine
estate, often with a masterly Muscat and
Rieslings with much breeding (also from
the Wineck-Schlossberg).
Meyer Fonne Rieslings from Kaefferkopf

and Schlossberg, Gewurztraminer Sch-
lossberg.
Philippe Klée Frequently crowned wi-
nes.
Victor Klée & Fils Be sure to ask to
taste the Riesling.
Klur-Stoeckle Produces expressive
Riesling and Gewurztraminer.

NIEDERMORSCHWIHR

Niedermorschwihr is romantically situated on a crossroads in a wine valley. The village, which was once the property of the Maltese Knights of St John, was heavily hit during the Second World War. Luckily, half the

The church has a spiral spire.

houses were spared, so one still sees many half-timbered houses, some with artistically worked corner posts. From late spring until well into autumn, almost all the residences are adorned with flowers and the fountain is also beautifully decorated.

The church is modern but is flanked by a striking, 13th century clock tower with a somewhat spiral-shaped steeple. This is the only one in Alsace. In the church, which is next to the city hall, one finds a Silbermann organ that has a covered, wooden outer staircase.

The well-sheltered Sommerberg is the local grand cru, known above all for its Rieslings. The name Niedermorschwihr comes from Morsvilre (first mentioned in 1214). This explains why the head of a Moor is contained in the village coat of arms.

The Sommerberg.

RECOMMENDED PRODUCERS
Albert Boxler & Fils Small wine estate with absolutely delicious wines. Situated at the western end of the main street. Muscat, Riesling, Riesling Sommerberg, Riesling Brand, Tokay Pinot Gris Sommerberg, Tokay Pinot Gris Brand, Gewurztraminer Brand.

Justin Boxler Riesling Brand with allure.
Marcel Mullenbach Runs a modest, fragmented property. Muscat, Riesling, Tokay Pinot Gris, Gewurztraminer.

RELATED TO WINE
• The local wine festival is usually organized in October.

HOTEL
Kuehn
℡ 89.27.38.38
Situated a few dozen
metres from the N 415
(which has four lanes at
that point). Its nearly 30
rooms are divided
among three floors. Pri-
ces: FF 250 to FF 280;
rural comfort. In the restaurant the cooking is
professional and inven-
tive. Some dishes are
dedicated to Pierre Ga-
ertner, the man who
made *Aux Armes de
France* (*sole au Gewurz-
traminer*) famous in
Ammerschwihr. Menus
start from FF 150.

RESTAURANT
Taverne Alsacienne
℡ 89.27.08.41
On the corner, near the
Fecht, one can eat well:
both the traditional as
well as the daring dis-
hes have style. Full choice of regional
wines. Menus from un-
der FF 100.

INGERSHEIM

At the foot of the Florimont grand cru – not only
famous for its Riesling and Gewurztraminer, but
also as a 'paradise for botanists' – lies the village of
Ingersheim. It is at least twelve centuries old, although this is not very noticeable as damage from
the war was extensive here.

Part of the village rampart is still intact and a few
parts of the Hexenturm still stand near a house in
the rue Maréchal Foch. The church has a medieval tower and is surrounded by an old embank-
ment. Ingersheim also has a Romanesque chapel
with a fine statue of the Virgin Mary. The former
city hall (rue de la République) was built in the
Renaissance style. Under the open clock tower
one may see the moustached heads of three Hun-
garian brothers: the present *mairie* was formerly a
residence and dates from the 18th century.
Ingersheim has more than 200 hectares of vineyards but it is still not really a wine village. It
functions mainly as a commuter area for Colmar;
they are separated from each other by the Fecht.

Most of
Ingersheim's
winegrowers
are affiliated
to the local
cooperative.

The city hall dates from the 18th century.

RECOMMENDED PRODUCERS
Cooperative The better wines from the
range nowadays include Pinot Blanc, Pi-
not Blanc Auxerrois, Riesling Steinweg,
Riesling Sommerberg, Gewurztraminer
Florimont, Gewurztraminer Cuvée Sainte-
Marguerite, Crémant.
Domaine Thomann A wine estate, run

by two brothers, with a fine Riesling and
Gewurztraminer from the Letzenberg.

RELATED TO WINE
• The village festival – which has wine as
its theme – usually takes place at the
end of August, or the beginning of September.

The restaurant Au Fer Rouge is situated in the old centre.

COLMAR

The French writer Voltaire, who resided in Colmar for almost one year in the middle of the 18th century, complained about the coffee but praised the wine. Colmar had been considered the wine capital of Alsace for hundreds of years. Many merchants were settled there; they shipped their wine on the Lauch, a tributary of the Ill, which flows into the Rhine north of Strasbourg. In earlier times, transport by water was much more important than by land, therefore Colmar had functioned as a shipping point for Alsatian wine ever since the 14th century.

Nowadays Colmar is, above all, the administra-

HOTEL
Hôtel de la Fecht
1 rue de la Fecht
✆ 89.41.34.08
Almost 40 stylish rooms within walking distance of the northern side of the old centre. Prices start at around FF 300. Also a restaurant. Book at the back if possible.

RECOMMENDED PRODUCERS
Institut National de la Recherche Agronomique (Inra) The private vineyards serve not only for experimentation, but also for the production of various good wines, including the Riesling and Gewurztraminer Cuvée des Catherinettes (28 rue de Herrlisheim).

Robert Karcher & Fils Wine estate with land on the Harth. From it come the Tokay Pinot Gris and Gewurztraminer Harth (11 rue de l'Ours).

↑ *Behind the Ancienne Douane a large market takes place every Saturday.*

tive centre for regional viniculture. There are also training and research institutes to be found here, and every year the largest wine exchange in Alsace is organized as well. Hardly any producers are established here, although one does find, just north of the city, a large, quite flat vineyard, the Harth. The land of the Harth is mainly in the hands of winegrowers and cooperatives from neighbouring districts. All in all, present-day Colmar is hardly worth a visit for its wines. The city itself is actually lovely – at any rate in the centre – but the suburbs are rather cluttered and are full of apartment blocks.

The only way to explore Colmar is by foot. Next

Rapp
1 rue Weinemer
✆ 89.41.62.10
Situated in the historic quarter, in a one-way street near the place Rapp. Around 40 neat rooms with varying facilities (starting from around FF 250). In the nearby restaurant one can eat extremely well.

Bernard Schoffit A passionate winegrower with perfect wines. The collection includes Chasselas, Sylvaner, Pinot Blanc, Muscat, Riesling and Gewurztraminer Harth, as well as striking wines from the Rangen in Thann: Riesling, Tokay Pinot Gris, Gewurztraminer (27 rue des Aubépines).

Domaine Viticole de la Ville de Colmar The wines of this municipal property come from the Clos Saint-Jacques in Colmar itself and from properties in nearby districts. The quality of the range is shown by the many awards it has won (2 rue Stauffen).

Saint-Martin
38 Grand'Rue
✆ 89.24.11.51
Despite the fact that it is situated in the centre, the rooms are still quite peaceful. Rural ambiance, old building. Prices start from FF 300.

Terminus-Bristol
7 place de la Gare
✆ 89.41.10.10
Traditional, solid city hotel with 70 comfortable, renovated rooms. Prices from FF 350. Also a restaurant.

RESTAURANTS

Au Fer Rouge
52 Grand'Rue
✆ 89.41.37.24
Creative, very modern cuisine in an especially fine half-timbered house. Be prepared for high prices: dinner menus start from FF 350. The lunch menu during the week costs more than FF 200.

Chez Hansi
23 rue des Marchands
✆ 89.41.37.84
Unpretentious winstub where Alsatian dishes are prepared with care and served by women in traditional costumes. A fine place to eat for *choucroute*. Menus from about FF 100.

The large church of Saint-Martin.

to the old city centre lies a large parking place, at the place Rapp (on the avenue de la République). The statue of General Rapp, an adjutant of Napoleon, is by Bartholdi. To the north and east of the place Rapp, close to ten small sidestreets lead to the historic quarter. It might be an idea to visit the Musée Unterlinden first. This 'Louvre of Alsace' can be reached by walking a little to the north, through the avenue de la République and the rue Kléber. In the latter street one passes Les Catherinettes, a former monastery church (rebuilt in the 18th century) which, despite its sombre appearance, serves as a reception room. The Unterlinden museum, which was founded in 1850, is situated in a 13th century Dominican monastery and lodges very old as well as ultra modern art. There is an unbelievable amount to be seen.

On the ground floor one finds much religious art in the form of medieval paintings, engravings and

RELATED TO WINE

• Colmar's large, regional wine exchange usually takes place in the first and second weeks of August on a large site next to the northern exit road in the direction of Strasbourg.

• The Comité Interprofessionnel du Vin d'Alsace is established in Colmar. One can contact this well-informed organization for every possible sort of data concerning Alsatian winegrowing. Address: Maison du Vin d'Alsace, 12, avenue de la Foire aux Vins (near the site of the wine exchange). ✆ 89.41.06.21.

altar pieces. The retable of Issenheim, in particular, is sublime; this dates from the 16th century and can be seen in the monastery chapel.

Other sections of the museum are devoted to archeological finds, statuary, wood carving and modern art (with, among others, paintings by Braque, Buffet, Monet, Picasso, Renoir). Also interesting is the cobbled wine cellar with its marvellous, decorated vats.

On the first floor, every conceivable object and work of art brings the history of Colmar and Alsace to life. Naturally, the work of Hansi is represented, the name under which Jean-Jacques Waltz (1873-1951) wrote, drew and painted. On one hand, he expressed, in a romantic way, the easy-going life of the Alsatians, on the other hand, he produced sharp caricatures of the German invaders. He was also curator of the Musée Unterlinden.

Coming from the museum one sees a crossing on the left, on the other side of the square. One of the streets leading from the crossing is the rue des Têtes. Here stands the Maison des Têtes. This merchant's house, dating from 1609, has numerous smirking heads on its stone façade, with, on top, a

A good place for sauerkraut.

S'Parisser Stewwele
4 place Jeanne d'Arc
✆ 89.41.42.33
It is with pleasure that the winegrowers of the city and its surroundings take their guests to this cosy winstub. Regional dishes based on ingredients fresh from the market, large wine list, reasonable prices. Located in a half-timbered house.

Schillinger
16 rue Stanislas
✆ 89.41.43.17
Classically furnished corner restaurant where the cooking is of an extremely high standard. Impressive wine cellar, which can be visited. The least expensive menu is about FF 350.

Courtyard next to a shopping street.

Tourist Tips

Tourist Tips
- On Saturday mornings, a large market is held in the centre (behind the Ancienne Douane).
- On the square behind the Ancienne Douane stands the Fontaine Schwendi. Here stands the statue of Lazare de Schwendi, the man who brought the pinot gris from Hungary to Alsace. In his right hand the figure holds a bunch of grapes. (See also Kientzheim.)
- As far as rain is concerned, Colmar is presumed to be the driest city in France after Perpignan.
- A marvellous collection of drawings, prints, paintings, posters and postcards by Hansi has been brought together in *Le grand livre de l'oncle Hansi* (Editions Herscher, Paris, 1982).

statue of a cooper by Bartholdi. Diagonally behind the Maison des Têtes lies the place des Dominicains (reached via, among others, the rue des Boulangers). The 14th century church that stands there has fine stained glass windows. Close by one finds a square with the large church of Saint-Martin (13th and 14th centuries).

On the southern side of this square runs one of Colmar's shopping streets: the rue des Marchands. On a corner of this street stands perhaps one of the most famous residences in Alsace, the Maison Pfister. This gem was built by a hat merchant from Besançon and was finished in 1537. The sandstone building has a corner bay window, wooden balconies, an octagonal ziggurat-like tower and is decorated with wall paintings and medallions. The other buildings in the rue des Marchands and sidestreets also have much style. In the rue des Marchands there is a splendid museum devoted to Bartholdi, the sculptor, who created among other works, the American Statue of Liberty.

The south end of the street leads to the Grand'Rue. Immediately on the right is the Ancienne Douane, a large building of which the oldest part dates from 1480. The multicoloured roof is of a later date. Behind this 'Koïfhus' lies a beautiful square which, via many small streets, gives access to the wonderfully restored Quartiers des Tanneurs and La Petite Venise, a romantic area of canals.

The famous Maison Pfister.→

HOTELS
Berceau du Vigneron
© 89.27.23.55
Ideally situated on the place Turenne. More than 15 stylish rooms. Prices start from FF 200. The hotel also runs a congenial *caveau*, at the start of the Grand'Rue, where the food and drink are good.

Les Vosges
© 89.27.02.37
A white building with a terrace, just outside the Porte de France. Around 30 tidy rooms without excessive luxuries. Prices from about FF 200. In the restaurant mainly regional dishes, which offer value for your money, are served. The smallest menu costs less than FF 100.

RESTAURANT
A l'Homme Sauvage
© 89.27.56.15
Talented chef, who cooks well and with imagination. The ambiance is Renaissance. Menus start from a low FF 150.

The Brand is the best known local vineyard.

TURCKHEIM

From Colmar, Niedermorschwihr, Wintzenheim and Munster, roads run to Turckheim, a small city in the Fecht valley. Due to its strategic position it was fortified at the beginning of the 14th century. Later, in and around Turckheim, there were frequent battles, for example during the Thirty Years' War and in 1675, when Henri de la Tour, Viscount of Turenne, with 20,000 men defeated an invading German army three times that strength. The Second World War has also left its mark here.

Despite all this violence, Turckheim has kept its charm and beauty. The fortifications have been demolished, but the triangular village still lies caught between three large, fortified gateways. From Colmar and Wintzheim one passes the

A romantic view.→

RECOMMENDED PRODUCERS
François Baur Petit-Fils/Domaine Langehald A wine estate where one can taste, among others, a Gewurztraminer Brand.

Cooperative Among others: the Pinot Blanc, Klevner, Tokay Pinot Gris, Tokay Pinot Gris Heimbourg, Muscat Heimbourg, Riesling Brand and Heimbourg, Gewurztraminer Brand and the Pinot Noir.

Auguste Hurst & Fils Very successful Riesling and Gewurztraminer Brand. The Pinot Noir is also of a high quality.

Charles Schleret Good reputation for wines such as Pinot Blanc, Muscat, Riesling, Tokay Pinot Gris and Gewurztraminer.

The Grand'Rue of Turckheim.

TOURIST TIP

• On summer evenings a night watchman makes his rounds at about 10:00 p.m. He sings to the inhabitants in dialect and wishes them a good night.

Porte de France, from Niedermorschwihr the Porte du Brand, from Munster the Porte de Munster. Near the latter the statue of Turenne stands. The best place to begin a stroll through Turckheim is the Porte de France, because directly behind this 14th century bulwark lies the most beautiful spot of the city, the place Turenne. To the left runs the Grand'Rue with its houses dating from the 16th and 17th centuries. Immediately to the right stands a half-timbered house of which the bay window is supported by a wooden pillar. Next to this building one finds a view of the Renaissance city hall with, behind it, a partially Romanesque church tower, while to the right a former guard and guild house, as well as the 18th century fountain Stockbrunna, can be seen. By walking a little further in the direction of the city hall, one comes to the Hôtel des Deux Clefs, a former inn that was restored in the 17th century.

Domaine Zind-Humbrecht Fine wines: Pinot d'Alsace, Pinot Noir, Muscat de Gueberschwihr, Tokay Pinot Gris; Rieslings from Gueberschwihr, Turckheim, Wintzenheim and, from the grands crus, Brand, Hengst, Clos Saint Urbain and Clos Windsbuhl.

RELATED TO WINE
• Directly to the north of Turckheim lie a series of wine hills which, together, form the Brand. A wine walk leads through the Brand.
• At the end of July Turckheim celebrates its wine festival.

The remains of a Roman resting place in the Hengst vineyard.

WINTZENHEIM

Just like Turckheim, Wintzenheim is situated in the valley of the Fecht, although on the south bank. The village has quite a few residential areas, because many people who work in nearby Colmar live here.

Wintzenheim stretches out along the busy D 417, which connects Colmar with Munster and Gérardmer. The main street and sidestreets contain various buildings from the 16th, 17th and 18th centuries. One of the most beautiful half-timbered houses stands in the rue des Laboureurs; on the façade is a wooden balcony with two pillars.

RESTAURANT
Au Bon Coin
✆ 89.27.48.04
This simple and rustically furnished eating house does honour to its name, because it is sitted on a corner by the city hall. Regional dishes are prepared here with love. There is often a fish dish with Riesling sauce and, when in season, game is served. The menus start under FF 100.

RECOMMENDED PRODUCERS
Josmeyer Small wine house which follows a stringent policy of quality. One of the specialities is Pinot Blanc; this can sometimes taste better than the Rieslings of less serious producers. The house makes various Pinots, including the Cuvée des Printemps, Les Lutins and Pinot Auxerrois H (from the Hengst). Other fine wines are the Rieslings Le Kottabe and Hengst, the Gewurztraminers Les Folatières and Hengst, Muscat Les Fleurons, Tokay Pinot Gris Cuvée du Centenaire, not forgetting the Chasselas H.

TOURIST TIPS
- On the west side of Wintzenheim, near to the D 417, stand the ruins of 13th century Château Pflixbourg. On the same side of the village, a winding path leads to the remains of the once powerful Château Hohlandsbourg. This also dates from the 13th century. It was rebuilt in the 16th century and dismantled in the 17th. The view is fantastic.
- For tea and cake or breakfast, the pâtisserie/tea salon near the village square is a good place to go.

A square along the main street functions as the centre of Wintzenheim. This is dominated by the neo-classical church (1849) and the city hall, which is sited in the former castle of Thurnbourg. The Fountain of the Holy Virgin (1756) is also to be found here. In a westerly direction further along the main street there stands a chapel.

The most famous vineyard of Wintzenheim is the

The village square with the Fountain of the Holy Virgin.

Hengst grand cru. This can be reached by driving in the direction of Colmar from the village square, then turning right at the first traffic light, left at the first ordinary street and afterwards keeping to the right. The way across the hilly Hengst is not only worthwhile because of the view across Colmar and Wettolsheim, but also because the remains of a Roman terminus dating from the 1st century lie here; three centuries later a look-out tower was added to it.

Bernard Staehlé Just like Josmeyer, it is established along the main street. Priceless Crémant. The best Riesling is Cuvée Dame Blanche.

le Galz

Katzenthal

Labaroche
Belvédère

les Trois Épis

Niedermorschwihr

Ungersheim

Cim. All.

Wicker

Horbourg-Wihr
-en-

Turckheim

Grinnack

976

Zimmerbach

Chât. de Pflixbourg

Wintzenheim

Walbach

COLMAR

PF

Sundhoffe

bach

Vallée de la Fecht

Ch Wettolsheim

Eguisheim

Tours d'Eguisheim

Herrlisheim-près-Colmar

Griesbach-au-Val

Soultzbach-les-Bains

Husseren-les-Châteaux

Voegtlinshofen

Obermorschwihr

Hattstatt

Ste-Croix-en-Plaine

Gueberschwihr

B. de Pfaffenheim

Pfaffenheim

552

Osenbach

F. de Westhalten

Oberhe

Wintzfelden

Ohmbach

375

Rouffach

Oberhe

Cim. Roumain

Bilzheim

Soultzmatt

Westhalten

Niederentze

Forêt de Schimberg

Vir

Oberentzen

Schweighouse

Orschwihr

Munwiller

Bergholtzzell

l'Oberlinger

573

Bergholtz

Gundolsheim

Guebwiller

SP

Merxheim

Meyenheim

Raguisheim

Cim. Fr.-All.

553

Ssenheim

Soultz-Haut-Rhin

Raedersheim

Ungersheim

Wuenheim

Cité

Hartmannswiller

Bollwiller

Feldkirch

le Vieil

Ensisheim

The smith's sign.

RESTAURANT
Auberge du Père Floranc
✆ 89.41.39.14
Tasty, regional dishes are the speciality of this famous inn, such as four sorts of *foie gras* and quail pie (*tourte de cailles*). The pink building has a dining room with a high wainscot and a marvellous wooden ceiling with triangular panels. The wine list is very extensive. Menus start from FF 200. The establishment has about 30 rooms at its disposal. The most peaceful are those at the rear, around the garden. Prices from about FF 300.

WETTOLSHEIM

Due to the fact that numerous articles from the Roman period have been excavated at Wettolsheim, it has been given the nickname 'Pompeii of Alsace'. The Roman villa that stood here was possibly even the cradle of Alsatian viniculture. Just like its neighbour Wintzenheim, the present village functions for a large part, as a dormitory suburb for Colmar. Winegrowing is also of importance, however, because this wine region has one of the largest surface areas.

Near to the village square, the quiet place Général de Gaulle, rises the slender tower of the church Saint-Rémy (1782). Inside is a painting that depicts the baptism of Clovis. On the square itself stands a fountain with a statue of Saint Nicolas on top. Only a few dozen metres further, in 1911, archbishop Schoepfer built a replica of the grotto at Lourdes. This stands on the street and is higher than the houses next to it.
The centre also con-

Replica of the grotto at Lourdes.

RECOMMENDED PRODUCERS
Domaine Barmès Buecher A star in the range is the Gewurztraminer Steingrubler. Other successes are Pinot Blanc, Tokay Pinot Gris (generic and Herrenweg), Riesling (generic, Herrenweg, Hengst) and the Gewurztraminer Hengst.
Paul Buecher & Fils A few generous

Gewurztraminers
Robert Dietrich Superior Tokay Pinot Gris Steingrubler.
François Ehrhart Impressive Gewurztraminers.
Albert Mann Extremely reliable winegrower. Pinot Blanc, Tokay Pinot Gris, Riesling, Riesling Schlossberg, Gewurz-

Saint Nicolas stands above the village fountain.

tains quite a few half-timbered houses. Various chapels and also a very early Feldkirch, which stood outside the village, have been lost in the course of the centuries. This also holds for the Château of Martinsbourg, where, in the 18th century, a romance took place between the Italian poet Alfieri and the Countess of Albany, married to Charles Edward, the last of the Stuarts. Grapevines have always existed in Wettolsheim, in particular on the sloping grand cru Steingrubler, where, above all, the Tokay Pinot Gris, Riesling and Gewurztraminer offer strikingly good quality.

TOURIST TIPS
- Across from the *Auberge du Père Floranc*, it is possible to buy young grapevines for your own garden.
- Hidden on a wooded mountain slope, behind Wettolsheim, stand the ruins of the 12th century Château de Hagueneck.

traminer Steingrubler.
Aimé Stentz The best wines that the family Stentz make include Muscat, Tokay Pinot Gris and Riesling Sommerberg.
Wunsch et Mann The most interesting creations are the Riesling and Tokay Pinot Gris Cuvée Joseph Mann, Riesling and Gewurztraminer Cuvée Saint-Rémy, Ge-

wurztraminer Hengst and sometimes a Muscat as well.

RELATED TO WINE
- The last Sunday of July is the day of the wine festival.
- Wettolsheim and the Beaujolais village of Fleurie are twinned with each other.

A small square behind the church.

EGUISHEIM

In the Unterlinden Museum in Colmar, the remains of *Homo egisheimiensis*, a Cro-Magnon, can be seen. These were discovered in 1865 at Eguisheim and prove that, tens of thousands of years ago, humans lived in this part of Alsace.

Yet more famous than this ancient forefather is Bruno of Eguisheim, the son of Count Hugon IV of Eguisheim and Countess Heilwige of Dabo. Bruno, who was later canonized, became the first and only Alsatian Pope, Léon IX (1048-1054). He was also a pope who brought about many reforms. The mighty dynasty of the counts of Eguisheim disappeared at the end of the 12th century, but their residence, the Château d'Eguisheim, still exists. This lies in the middle of the village, on a small square, wedged in by houses. The building, originally dating from 720, was radically renovated in 1894 and since that time has had a multicoloured spire. The same holds for the roof of the chapel next to it. The oldest part is the octagonal stone wall surrounding the hill upon which the complex was built long ago. This wall has been declared a monument. On the square in front of it stands a statue of Léon IX. After being destroyed in the 15th century, Eguis-

HOTELS

Auberge Alsacienne
✆ 89.41.50.20
This hotel, with its 19 rooms, is located in an old building along the Grand'Rue. The interior is neat and simple. Some rooms bear the names of wines; most are situated peacefully at the rear. Prices average about FF 230. Also a restaurant. Unfortunately the service is often

RECOMMENDED PRODUCERS

Charles Baur Succ This winegrowing family, located in the Grand'Rue, has in its selection a Muscat and Riesling Eichberg, as well as a Gewurztraminer Pfersigberg.

Léon Baur & Fils One of the specialities of Jean-Louis Baur is his Riesling Cuvée

Elisabeth Stumpf.

Léon Beyer In general the wines taste quite firm. A few recommended names are: Pinot Blanc, Muscat Réserve, Tokay Pinot Gris Réserve and Cuvée Particulière, Riesling Les Ecailliers and Cuvée Particulière, Gewurztraminer Cuvée des Comtes d'Eguisheim.

heim was rebuilt and received its present, unique form, namely that, around the castle, the streets were set out in three oval, defensive rings. On their outer side – where the enemy was expected – these ramparts are tight, sober and severe, but on the inner side they appear very sweet, with flowers everywhere, façade decorations, colourful hatches, bay windows and wooden balconies. One of the most beautiful walks in the whole of Alsace is through the street ramparts of Eguisheim. Cars are hardly ever seen: for about one hour one travels back hundreds of years in time. The highest monument within the ramparts is the clock tower dating from 1220, with, beneath it, a chapel in which the former church portal

not exactly cheery, which makes this an establishment to be visited only if nowhere else is available.

Hostellerie du Pape
& 89.41.41.21
Tastefully designed complex with 33 rooms that have modern comforts (T.V., mini-bar, hair-dryer, etc.). Prices start from about FF 400. Also a restaurant (menus begin under FF 100) and caveau. Sited in the Grand'Rue, near the entrance of the village.

The picturesque ramparts.

Luc Beyer Has cellars on the place du Château. Riesling Pfersigberg.
Cooperative The range is large. The simpler wines are scarcely worth attention, but there are also very good wines. These include Rieslings such as those of the Hengst and Steingrubler, Tokay Pinot Gris from the Eichberg and Steingrubler, Gewurztraminer from the Eichberg, Hengst Pfersigberg and Steingrubler, and the Pinot Noir Cuvée de la Prince Hugo. The allied Domaine Jux puts a good Riesling, Tokay Pinot Gris and Gewurztraminer onto the market.
Joseph Freudenreich & Fils Successful Muscat and Gewurztraminer.

RESTAURANTS
Caveau d'Eguisheim

℗ 89.41.08.89

On the first floor of this winstub one eats Alsatian dishes in an Alsatian ambiance. The *choucroute* here is famous. Many local wines. Menus start at about FF 150. No one can miss the large 18th century winepress.

La Grangelière

℗ 89.23.00.30

The former chef of the Château d'Isenbourg (Rouffach) cooks to a high standard here. The dishes are often rich in flavour and reasonably modern in character, such as *osso bucco* made of wolffish with horseradish sauce. There is also *choucroute* (for about FF 100). Stylish interior with cheerful curtains.

S'Wenzer Stewla

℗ 89.24.01.90

Friendly waitresses wear traditional costumes in this winstub, and usually the *patron* does as well. Rural, reasonably priced regional dishes and wines from the private wine estate of the families Zinck-Feuermann.

The courtyard of a wine producer.

(with a Romantic typanum) can be admired. The church itself dates from 1807; its modern stained glass windows relate the life of Léon IX.

A few steps west of the clock tower stands one of the six tithe barns of Eguisheim. On this *cours dimières*, the monastic orders and the archbishop of Strasbourg (who furnished Eguisheim with its first ramparts, later demolished) collected the obligatory contributions from the inhabitants. It was not uncommon to settle this in wine, because the wine history of Eguisheim goes back to Roman times (which

Along the ramparts.

Paul Ginglinger Talented farmer with fine grands crus: Riesling and Gewurztraminer.

Pierre-Henri Ginglinger Get to know the delicious Crémant, while the Gewurztraminer Eichberg is also not to be spurned.

Albert Hertz Eichberg wines in the variants Riesling, Tokay Pinot Gris, Gewurztraminer. Also good are the generic Riesling and Gewurztraminer.

Bruno Hertz Pinot Blanc, Muscat, Tokay Pinot Gris.

Bruno Sorg Flawless wines with much charm. For instance: Muscat Pfersigberg, Riesling and Gewurztraminer Florimont.

also holds for neighbouring Wettolsheim). A number of streets very appropriately bear the names of grape varieties, such as Rue du Riesling, Rue du Tokay. Centuries ago, the wines of Eguisheim were already being served at the courts

A shop on the church square.

LE PAVILLON GOURMAND
ⓒ 89.24.36.88
Small, tastefully decorated and furnished restaurant in an old half-timbered house. Local cuisine, reasonably priced (menu within FF100).

TOURIST TIPS
- On the place du Marché (centre, near the castle) stands a beautiful 16th century fountain.
- For the Tours d'Eguisheim – three massive fortified towers on a mountain peak above the village – see Husseren-les-Châteaux.

of England and Holland and, during his stay in Colmar, Voltaire, who gladly drank wine, bought land here.

To each side and behind Eguisheim, the vineyards lie like a green blanket draped over the foothills of the nearby Vosges. Two fields have the status of grand cru: Eichberg and Pfersigberg. Both are famous for their Gewurztraminers, but tokay pinot gris, riesling and muscat also appear to thrive here.

Streets with the names of grapes.

Antoine Stoffel Small winegrower with a house and cellars in a modern quarter. Pinot Auxerrois, Riesling, Muscat, Tokay Pinot Gris, Gewurztraminer, Gewurztraminer Eichberg, Pinot Noir. Actually everything here tastes good.

RELATED TO WINE

- Usually in the last weekend of March, a festival is held in which producers present and open their wines for evaluation of the previous harvest.
- The day of the annual Fête des Vignerons is the last Sunday of August.

Husseren's striking hotel.

**HOTEL
Husseren-les-Châteaux**
℡ 89.49.22.93
This is one of the most striking hotels of the entire Alsace. It stands against a wooded hill above the village and consists of 38 maisonettes with, downstairs, a comfortable sitting room plus bathroom, and, upstairs, the sleeping quarters. The interior is dominated by white tints and is not at all typically French in appearance, many articles

HUSSEREN-LES-CHATEAUX

Husseren-les-Châteaux is the highest wine village of Alsace. It is situated three kilometres from Eguisheim, against a slope and in the middle of vineyards, at a height of 380 metres. Here the workers who built the castles for the counts of Eguisheim lived. When the hamlet achieved its independence in the 14th century, the inhabitants did not receive enough land to live by. As a result, until the last century Husseren had more distillers than winegrowers, because one could earn more from the berries from the nearby forests than could be earned through winegrowing.
Nowadays, however, winegrowing is extremely

RECOMMENDED PRODUCERS
Alphonse Kuentz Among others, two delicious wines from the Pfersigberg, a Riesling and Gewurztraminer.
Kuentz-Bas The Riesling Réserve Personnelle has breeding, distinction and, in its youth, is already delicious, while those of the Grands Crus Eichberg and Pfersig-

berg ask for a few years' patience. The Pinot Blanc, Muscat, Tokay Pinot Gris, Pinot Noir Réserve Personnelle, the Gewurztraminers Eichberg and Pfersigberg, the sparkling Brut de Chardonnay and the *cuvées* have unmistakable class.
Edouard Leibner Tokay Pinot Gris. Taste the Pinot Blanc and Gewurztraminer.

important. In the village a trend-setting wine house and about 20 independent winegrowers are situated; most have a sign on the façade. The wines of Husseren are of a high quality because all the grapevines are sited against slopes.

The most attractive element of the village is its panoramic view across Eguisheim and the wide landscape; it is no coincidence that the Romans had a watchpost here. The Neo-Gothic church of Saint-Pancrace (1885) contains a 16th century statue of the saint and a 12th century baptismal font, originally from the abbey of Murbach.

Most visitors are attracted to quiet Husseren on the weekend after the 14th of July, because then they celebrate the Fête des Guingettes d'Europe, with food and drink stalls from all over of Europe and performances by international song and dance groups.

having come from Denmark. It is run by two couples who, together, make up three nationalities: Danish, German and Dutch. This most peacefully situated hotel also offers a covered, shallow swimming pool, a playroom for children, a tennis court and other facilities. In its restaurant one can feast on a sublime *terrine de foie de canard* and other classic dishes which often also have a modern touch. Many wines from the village itself. Room prices start at around FF 400, menus from about FF 100.

TOURIST TIP

- On the mountain top at Husseren stand the Tours d'Eguisheim, three fortified towers that are the remains of castles probably dating from the 11th to the 13th centuries. From north to south they are called Dagsbourg, Wahlenbourg and Weckmund. Beautiful panoramic view.

Kuentz-Bas offers first class wines.

Eugène Lichtlé & Fils More than average Pinot Noir and Tokay Pinot Gris.
François Lichtlé Pleasing Crémant, sultry, spicy Gewurztraminer.
André Scherer Muscat Cuvée Jean Baptiste, Riesling and Gewurztraminer Pfersigberg, Gewurztraminer Eichberg.
Gérard Schueller Stimulating Riesling

with much breeding, distinctive Tokay Pinot Gris.
Emile Schwartz & Fils Modest property. The ordinary, as well as the Gewurztraminer Pfersigberg,is of a high quality.
Fernand Stentz Riesling Cuvée des Buis, Riesling Pfersigberg. Surprisingly good Pinot Blanc. Wood-matured Pinot Noir.

VOEGTLINSHOFEN

From Husseren-les-Châteaux, the wine route runs gradually downwards with some bends; to the east along the way, one can admire a magnificent view across the Rhine valley. Voegtlinshofen is the next village. Almost all the houses along the main street bear gable signs and signboards of winegrowers, while, around a bend, two enormous bottles stand on either side of an entrance gate. Nowadays little Voegtlinshofen is a real wine village, although the wine history here is actually shorter than in many other places, because it was not until 1887 that the inhabitants received their own land. Before this poverty ruled: the popula-

The present village dates from the 17th and 18th centuries.

RECOMMENDED PRODUCERS
Joseph Cattin & ses Fils Names to remember are the Muscat, Riesling, Tokay Pinot Gris and Gewurztraminer from the Hatschbourg, as well as the Crémant.
Théo Cattin & Fils The best generic wines are offered as Cuvée de l'Ours Noir (Pinot Blanc, Muscat, Gewurztraminer

and suchlike). Moreover, the assortment also offers a few wines of the Grands Crus. These include Muscat and Tokay Pinot Gris Hatschbourg, Gewurztraminer Bollenberg.
Gérard et Serge Hartmann Delicious Muscat. From the Hatschbourg they make a Tokay Pinot Gris and Gewurztraminer.

tion worked, for the most part, in nearby stone pits. The first local church was consecrated by the archbishop of Basel in 1145. In 1636, during the Thirty Years' War, the Swedish invaded the village. They caused enormous

Winegrowers live in almost all the houses.

destruction and the entire population fled. It was not until 1660 that people came to settle here once again. Many of them were Swiss immigrants, with typical Swiss names such as Cattin. The present church dates from 1788; like its predecessor, it is named after Saint Nicolas. The interior is richly decorated and contains a few lovely altars dating from 1704. Naturally, the annual village festival of Voegtlinshofen falls on December 6, Saint Nicolas's name day.

There are many Swiss names.

wer (with a half-timbered floor) in the 18th century church of Saint-Philippe et Saint-Jacques. On the little square near the church a gilded statue of the Virgin Mary stands above a fountain. In the church one finds wall paintings.
• Slightly to the northwest of Voegtlinshofen, there once stood the important Augustinian abbey of Marbach, the influence of which stretched across the whole of Europe. Of the 12th century structure only the ruins and a garden remain. These can be reached via a small path.

André Hartmann & Fils A series of beautiful wines. Muscat, Riesling, Tokay Pinot Gris (in various categories, including Armoirie), Tokay Pinot Gris Goldert, Gewurztraminer Hatschbourg.
Denis Meyer/Domaine Kehren Among others, Riesling Réserve Saint-Ulrich, Tokay Pinot Gris Cuvée Fernand, Gewurztra-miner Hatchbourg.

RELATED TO WINE
• A speciality of Voegtlinshofen is Muscat.
• The village has a grand cru, the Hatschbourg. It owes its reputation to its Muscat, Tokay Pinot Gris and Gewurztraminer.

A view of Gueberschwihr from Voegtlinshofen.

 HOTEL
Le Relais du Vignoble
℗ 89.49.22.22
This building, which lies just outside the old centre, was finished in 1975. On both sides of the red hallway there are 33 smart and very comfortable rooms. Those on the first floor have a balcony. Average room price FF 250 to 300. There are also bridal suites. The restaurant – which is called Belle-Vue – mainly offers regional specialities; the least expensive

GUEBERSCHWIHR

While villages such as Riquewihr, Kaysersberg and, to a lesser degree, Eguisheim have become very commercialized under the influence of tourism, Gueberschwihr is well-nigh untainted – and at least as beautiful. As its three gateways show, it was once fortified. What's more, there were once castles within the ramparts: Mittelbourg and Nortgasse (the remains may still be seen).

Winegrowers since 1620.

RECOMMENDED PRODUCERS
Ernest Burn This winegrower is the sole owner of the Clos Saint-Imer on the Goldert grand cru. Here, sublime wines are made: Muscat, Riesling, Tokay Pinot Gris, Gewurztraminer.
Lucien Gantzer Top wines: the Muscat, Riesling and Gewurztraminer.

Bernard Humbrecht Muscat, Riesling (generic and Goldert), Gewurztraminer Goldert.
Marcel Humbrecht There are also delicious Goldert wines here: Muscat, Riesling, Gewurztraminer.
Fernand Lichtlé Muscat and Gewurztraminer Goldert.

Thanks to winegrowing, Gueberschwihr flour-ished in the 16th century. Most of the houses date from this period and the two preceding centuries. Half-timbered houses, as well as buildings in the Renaissance style, can be seen here. The streets in the old centre are not only picturesque, but also narrow. The very broad village square, over which a tall lime tree casts its shadow, is in sharp con-trast.

Around the square various winegrowers are locat-ed, such as Bernard Humbrecht and Clément

menu costs less than FF 100. The *foie gras maison* is often sold along with a glass of *grains nobles* from their own wine estate, Do-maine Scherb.

TOURIST TIP

• Although it is not clearly indicated, it is possible to drive straight through the vineyards to Pfaffen-heim. This route is much more attractive via the N 83.

Weck, and the church, with its mag-nificent Romanesque clock tower, also stands there. This is the most impressive tower of its type in the region. It has three floors, was built in 1120 and is nowa-days the abode of hundreds of pigeons. The original church was replaced in the 19th century by the present, Neo-Roman-

The Romanesque clock tower.

tic one. Beside the tower there is a small chapel with a wrought-iron fence.

Gueberschwihr lies at the foot of the Heidenhöhle cliff; on the northern side of the village generous Gewurztraminers, aromatic Muscats and other noble wines come from the Goldert grand cru.

Louis Scherb & Fils Pinot Auxerrois, Muscat, Riesling Goldert, Gewurztraminer and other successful wines.
Maurice Schueller Muscat and Ge-wurztraminer Goldert.
Clément Weck Muscat and Gewurztra-miner Goldert. Premises on the village square.

RELATED TO WINE
• Usually, the wine cellars of Guebersch-wihr are open for visitors on the next-to-last Sunday of August. In the village there is singing and dancing, while many inhabitants wear traditional cos-tumes. The festival is called Fête de l'Amitié.

PFAFFENHEIM

From the north, Pfaffenheim can be reached in two ways: via the N 83 or via the vineyards. By first driving straight from the *route nationale* and thereafter keeping to the left, one will arrive at the place de la Mairie. The road through the vineyards also ends here.

This square offers parking facilities for a visit to the nearby church of Saint-Martin. This is flanked by a very modern, white concrete clock tower dating from 1976, but has a Romanesque choir. On the outside of this there are many notches. These were made by farmers in past times, who attempted to drive the devil from their sickles and other tools by striking them against these walls.

From behind the church one may enjoy a fine view across the rising vineyards. Not far to the

RESTAURANT
Au Petit Pfaffenheim
℡ 89.49.62.06
Despite its unpropitious location – next to the N 83, where the cooperative is also situated – this is a good place to eat. In the spacious dining room Alsatian dishes, including *schiffala* (smoked pork) with salads, *choucroute* and game, are cheerfully served at reasonable prices. Most of the menus cost less than FF 100. Also has a few rooms.

↑ *Notches made by scythes on the church.*
← *A wine cellar inundated with flowers.*

RECOMMENDED PRODUCERS
Cooperative A few of the good wines are: Edelzwicker, Pinot Blanc, Pinot Blanc Schneckenberg, Muscat Cuvée Diane, Muscat Goldert, Tokay Pinot Gris in the variants Cuvée Rabelais, Goldert and Steinert, Riesling Goldert, Gewurztraminer Goldert and Steinert, Crémant.

Pierre Frick Works without herbicides. His wines excel through their purity and charm. Pinot Blanc, Klevner, Riesling, Riesling Iris, Riesling Steinert, Muscat, Tokay Pinot Gris, Gewurztraminer (generic and Steinert).
Joseph Rieflé & Fils Among the better wines are Pinot Blanc, Muscat, Riesling

TOURIST TIP
- On the wooded mountain high above Pfaffenheim stands the chapel of Notre-Dame du Schauenberg. The way to it leads first through vineyards, thereafter through a mountain forest; the last part must be done on foot. From this pilgrim chapel (which has a Gothic choir) one can enjoy a spectacular panoramic view.

north of the church lies the tiny place Notre-Dame. The *Caveau Saint-Michel* on this square is charmingly decorated with multicoloured flowers, ivy and human figures in painted wood. Elsewhere along the winding streets of Pfaffenheim one will find various old wells and four fountains. If

The village has a wine walk.

you visit the village in springtime you will often hear the clinking of bottles, because this is when the young wine is bottled; at least one-third of approximately 1100 inhabitants earn their living from wine. Some of the streets are named after grapes, such as Rue du Muscat. The Steinert grand cru, which lies within the district of Pfaffenheim, is mainly known for its Tokay Pinot Gris – which is not to say that there are no other wines of distinction.

Tokay Pinot Gris is a local speciality.

Gaentzbrunnen, Tokay Pinot Gris, Gewurztraminer Steinert, Crémant.
François Runner Charming Pinot Noir. The Riesling and Gewurztraminer are also tasty.

RELATED TO WINE
- Pfaffenheim has a *sentier viticole*. This

walk through the vineyards lasts about one and a half hours (departure point place de la Mairie). During the harvest it is forbidden to walk it.
- On the second weekend of July the village celebrates its Fête des Caves. The local wines can be tasted to one's heart's content at the producers.

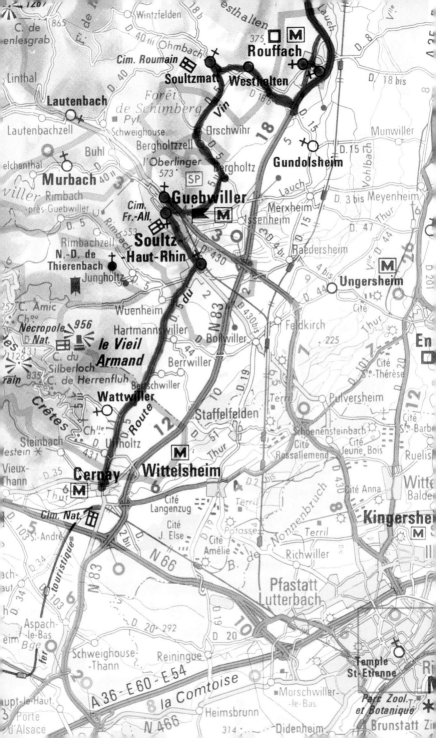

HOTELS
Château d'Isenbourg
© 89.78.53.70
On the foundations of a medieval fortress, a much more elegant castle was built in the 19th century. Only the vaulted cellars from the 15th century – where the restaurant is situated – remind one of the fortress of olden times. The business is a member of the prestigious group Relais & Château. Luxurious rooms starting from about FF 650. Private park, swimming pool and other excellent facilities. The cuisine for the pampered clientèle is very good and often inventive. Large choice of wines, including private wine estate wines. Menus from about FF 250.

The luxurious Château d'Isenbourg hotel.

ROUFFACH

Hidden behind a double-ring-wall and protected by the Château d'Isenbourg, Rouffach grew into a prosperous provincial town. For centuries this was the possession of the archbishops of Strasbourg, until, in 1238, Rouffach received its town franchise. That a long period of prosperity was enjoyed here is clear from the number of important monuments. Most of them stand on the spacious place de la République.

Construction of the church of Notre-Dame de l'Assomption took a long time, from the 11th to the 19th century. Therefore it is in part Romanesque and in part Gothic – while the southern tower was never completed. The front is mainly 14th century, with a rose window. Various art styles are also present in the vaulted interior, which glows with coloured light via a wonderful stained glass window.

RECOMMENDED PRODUCERS
Bruno Hunold There are very few independent winegrowers in Rouffach. One of them is Bruno Hunold, who receives his visitors in the rue au Quatre Vents. Riesling, Gewurztraminer Vorbourg.
Lycée Agricole et Viticole de Rouffach Behind the former city hall, on the eastern side of the ramparts, wine is produced by students of this school. The quality of the wines proves that the training here is of a high standard. Riesling, Gewurztraminer Vorbourg.
Muré Run a business firm, but also make wines from their own Clos Saint-Landelin, a terraced vineyard

Notre-Dame de l'Assomption.

Across from the church stands the former Corn Exchange (end 15th century) which has a stepped gable and is entered via a double staircase at the front. The former city hall, a building in the Renaissance style with two elegant gables, is also on the square. At the back of it stands the fortified Witch Tower with 13th and 15th century crenellation, a peaked roof and a stork's nest.

It is worth the effort to take a short walk in the Vieux Quartier (around the rue de la Poterie, beside the Corn Exchange) and over the former ramparts (behind the Witch Towers). Along the rue Poincaré, which runs directly through Rouffach, one will see a few fine bay windows, as well as the 13th century Franciscan church.

A la Ville de Lyon
℡ 89.49.65.51
More than 40 rooms, which run far to the rear. They are neat, but not all supply modern comfort. Prices: FF 315 to 350. In an additional building, a large brasserie and a stylishly furnished speciality restaurant are found.
A talented chef, Philippe Bohrer, cooks with great skill and the service is very pleasant. Menus start from about FF 110.

TOURIST TIP

• Rouffach has an 18-hole golf course east of the city.

The Witch Tower with its stork's nest.

within the Vorbourg grand cru. While the ordinary wines are generally of very decent to good quality (Gewurztraminer Zinnkoepflé), the show is stolen by the Muscat, Riesling, Tokay Pinot Gris, Gewurztraminer and wood-matured Pinot Noir from the Clos Saint-Landelin. Versions of these wines are regularly made with the predicate vendange tardive.

RELATED TO WINE

• The only grand cru of Rouffach is the Vorbourg grand cru.
• The large Foire Eco-Biologique of bread, wine and cheese takes place annually during the weekend of Ascension.

Westhalten is surrounded by three wine hills.

HOTEL
Domaine du Bollen-berg
© 89.49.62.47
This establishment was extended in the 1980s to make 50 rooms. These pleasant rooms are functionally furnished. Guests are assured of peace here, because the hotel stands in the middle of a wine estate on

The cooperative.

WESTHALTEN

Little Westhalten lies nestled in a valley which is enclosed by three wine hills: the Bollenberg, Strangenberg and Zinnkoepflé. Not only grape-vines but also very differing plants, amongst which even mediterranean sorts, thrive in the warm microclimate. Botanists have discovered no less than 550 southern French varieties, in particular on the Zinnkoepflé. These have been declared protected nature reserves.

Coming from the N 83 one gets a pleasant impres-sion of Westhalten and its location. Behind the decor of green wine hills rise the grey peaks of the Vosges, sometimes bedecked with snow.

The main street runs to the town hall, where

RECOMMENDED PRODUCERS
Cooperative Wine with a good average quality, such as Edelzwicker, Pinot Blanc Strangenberg, Sylvaner Comtes d'Alsace, Muscat, Riesling Zinnkoepflé, Gewurztra-miner from Zinnkoepflé and Vorbourg. The cooperative has taken over the local Heim wine house. The range of wines with this name also have quality, for example, wines such as Pinot Blanc (generic and Clos du Strangenberg), Riesling (diverse *cuvées* such as Les Eglantiers), Muscat, Gewurztraminer Zinnkoepflé, Crémant.
Diringer Family wine estate with two ex-cellent wines from the Zinnkoepflé: Ries-ling and Gewurztraminer.

The church of Saint-Blaise.

there is an old well (16th century) plus a fountain (17th century). By turning right one arrives in a street running upwards with the most beautiful house of the village; this is easily recognized by its stone bay window. Slightly further up stands, on the left hand, the church of Saint-Blaise, a Neo-Classical building from 1837. Almost directly afterwards the way runs into the vineyards. On the top of a hill, at a crossing, one has a delightful view from various sides. Colmar can be seen to the north, Westhalten and Ohrschwihr to the south.

By taking the same way back and turning right at the *mairie*, one drives with a few turnings through the rest of the main street, in order to come out eventually at the road to Soultzmatt and the important local cooperative.

The Zinnkoepflé.

the Bollenberg (watch for signposts along the N 83, south of Rouffach). Prices start at about FF 300. In the rustically decorated restaurant, *Au Vieux Pressoir*, regional dishes are served as well as their own wines (Clos Sainte-Apolline) and distillates. Dinner menus start at FF 200; less expensive lunch menu (during the week).

RESTAURANT
Au Cheval Blanc
℡ 89.47.01.16
The dining room is comfortable and there is a delicious aroma of cooking. The food here, based on ingredients fresh from the market, is good and very elegant. A number of the wines come from their own wine estate. The menus begin at around FF 150. In a peacefully situated building behind the restaurant, built in 1989, there are a dozen pleasant, light hotel rooms. Prices FF 350 to 400.

A. Wischlen Among others, Riesling, Tokay Pinot Gris Zinnkoepflé, Gewurztraminer Zinnkoepflé.

RELATED TO WINE
• Westhalten has a *sentier* which runs in part through vineyards and in part through Mediterranean flora. The starting point (with a parking area) is not far from the village centre. Once a week, from July to September, a guided walk takes place. The tour begins at 2:00 p.m., lasts one and a half hours and is brought to a close with wine tasting. Departure in front of the Caisse Mutuelle.

⚲ **HOTEL**
A la Vallée Noble
℅ 89.47.65.65

This rather new hotel is situated on a hill in a valley, about one kilometre west of the village. It has the appearance of a Swiss chalet. The rooms have balconies and are well equipped. That it is peaceful here speaks for itself. Prices around FF 300. A swimming pool, sauna and a gymnasium are available. The restaurant's speciality is snails.

RESTAURANT
Hotel-Restaurant
Klein
℅ 89.47.00.10

A cosy village restaurant with a dining room on each side of the entrance. Inviting bill of fare, extensive wine list. The cuisine is classíc and very well presented. The menus begin at approximately FF 100. The hotel has seven rooms at its disposal. Klein is sited oppsite the town hall.

SOULTZMATT

Following on from Westhalten, at the foot of the Zinnkoepflé grand cru, lies Soultzmatt. This elongated village is built along the valley of the Ohmbach. At the start of the village the Ohmbach runs past houses dating from the 16th and 17th centuries.

The Ohmbach in Soultzmatt.

A few hundred metres further up, on the left, stands the Château Wagenbourg. This dates from the beginning of the 16th century but was later rebuilt. The small garden has been laid out *à la française*. The building is the property of a winegrowing family.
Further into the village, just to the right of the main street, one finds the church of Saint-Sébastien with its Romanesque clock tower. In the tower one may see the gigantic clock, while,

Château Wagenbourg.

RECOMMENDED PRODUCERS
Léon Boesch & Fils Not only the Crémant, but various other sorts of wine from this family are also worth discovering, such as the Muscat, Riesling Vallée Noble, Tokay Pinot Gris and Gewurztraminer Zinnkoepflé.

Seppi Landmann Reliable name due to his simple wines (such as Sylvaner) and also to his grands crus (such as Riesling and Gewurztraminer Zinnkoepflé). The Crémant makes a delicious appetizer.
Château Wagenbourg Exceptionally pleasurable wines, among which the Pinot Blanc, Riesling and Gewurztraminer

The hôtel de ville with the Zinnkoepflé behind it.

inside the church the 15th century monument to Guillaume Kappler is very impressive.

The large town hall, which stands on a small square to the right along the main street, has angels on top of its gable and grapevines against it, as well as a striking tower. Next to the present *mairie* stands an old one, which is much smaller and can be recognized by its gabled roof and small tower spire.

Not far from the square there is a large map of the village. This also forms the departure point of Soultzmatt's wine promenade. On the west side of the village there are factories where mineral water from local sources is bottled: here one can taste not only wine but also water.

TOURIST TIP
- To the southwest of Soultzmatt stands the chapel of Notre-Dame du Schaefertal, which was once a place of pilgrimage. The small building dates from 1511 and was restored in 1950. There is also an interesting cloister in the neighbourhood.

can be tasted in a small annexe to this castle.

RELATED TO WINE
- The terrain of the large Zinnkoepflé grand cru lies within both Westhalten and Soultzmatt and gives many full-bodied, strong wines. Above all, the Ge-

wurztraminer and Tokay Pinot Gris can be exceptionally successful.
- Every Saturday between the 1st of July and the 1st of September a guided walk along the *sentier viticole* takes place. It lasts about two hours and is followed by wine tasting. Departure time about 1:30 p.m. at the town hall.

RESTAURANT
Caveau d'Orschwihr
℡ 89.76.90.31
Congenial place for lunch, where the cuisine is unpretentious and reasonably priced. Situated on the nicest square of the village, the place Saint-Nicolas.

TOURIST TIPS
• By following the wine route in a southerly direction, one arrives almost immediately in the neighbouring village of Bergholtz-Zell. The church here was

ORSCHWIHR

The history of Orschwihr certainly dates back to the 8th century. One of its oldest buildings is the Château d'Orschwihr. This dates from the 11th century and was inhabited by Pope Léon IX (see Eguisheim). Two fires, the last of which was in 1934, damaged it very badly. To this day parts of a wall, an arched bridge across the dry moat and cellars remain, which are used by a winegrower. Next to the castle stands the church. This was constructed in 1782 and is named after the local patron saint, Saint Nicolas. The outside of the building looks rather sober but it has a rich interior.

Orschwihr seen from the Bollenberg.

RECOMMENDED PRODUCERS
ORSCHWIHR
Lucien Albrecht Riesling Clos Himmelreich and Pfingstberg, Gewurztraminer Cuvée Martine, Tokay Pinot Gris and Gewurztraminer Pfingstberg, Crémant.
François Braun et ses Fils Riesling Bollenberg.

Château d'Orschwihr Pinot Noir Bollenberg, Gewurztraminer.
Materne Haegelin et Filles Among others, the Tokay Pinot Gris Cuvée Elise.
Raymond Rabold & Fils Generic Riesling and the Riesling Pfingstberg.
Vignobles Reinhart Riesling Bollenberg, Tokay Pinot Gris Cuvée Charlotte,

Wine can be tasted in abundance.

The very first church of Orschwihr stood high above the village, on the wine hill of Bollenberg. Nowadays one will find a chapel there. The path to it runs upwards from the church, between grapevines. The view from the chapel is panoramic. The Bollenberg is also the spot where, half way through August, the Haxafir is set up; the flames of this 15 metre high pyre are intended to drive off witches and demonic spirits before the harvest.

The centre of Orschwihr consists mainly of quiet streets with Renaissance houses dating from the 16th and 17th centuries. Most of them are inhabited by winegrowers. In the documents of the archbishop of Strasbourg, as well as other archives, the wines of Lippelsberg in particular, both the white and the red, are mentioned as far back as the 16th century. Even now the self-same vineyard is one of the best of Orschwihr, although it does not have the status of a grand cru. That privilege is meted out only to the Pfingstberg.

built in 1874 using, among other features, the pillars of a former Romanesque church. It was consecrated at the time by Pope Léon IX.

- To the southwest of Bergholtz-Zell lies the Garden of Oelberg, a pilgrimage centre with three chapels, two oratories and the Stations of the Cross (19th century).
- After Bergholtz-Zell the route runs temporarily through the flat terrain of the parish of Bergholtz. This is a rather boring village, even though the church tower bears a pink and white cupola. The most beautiful houses are located next to the church.

The chapel on the Bollenberg.

Gewurztraminer and other fine wines.
Jean-Michel Welty Gewurztraminers with much character.
Valentin Zusslin Aromatic Muscat Cuvée Maxie, superior Tokay Pinot Gris Cuvée Jean-Paul.
BERGHOLTZ
Jean-Pierre Dirler Clean, elegant wines.

Sylvaner Vieilles Vignes, Muscat, Muscat Saering, Riesling of Kessler as well as Saering and Spiegel, Gewurztraminer Spiegel, wood-ripened Pinot Noir.

RELATED TO WINE
- Harvest festival on the first weekend of October.

The Saint-Léger with its three towers.

RESTAURANT
La Taverne du Vigne-ron
✆ 89.76.81.89
This winstub may be found diagonally behind the Saint-Léger church, beside the tourist bureau. Regional cuisine, rustic ambiance with a beamed ceiling, modest prices (various menus below FF 100).

GUEBWILLER

In the 8th century Guebwiller was first mentioned as Gebunvillare. Thereafter the village was bound to the powerful abbey of Murbach for hundreds of years during which time the fortifications were constructed. According to reports, Brigitte Schick fended off a surprise attack on the ramparts by the Armagnacs on the 14th of Febuary, 1445.

Guebwiller honours this event by holding a special service in the Saint-Lèger on Saint Valentines Day. This large Romanesque church has three towers (one of which is placed at the crossing), a façade that is, rather unusually, crowned with a triangle of window panes and has marvellous woodwork in the choir. Against the arch of the right aisle, hang ropes and wooden ladders which

The main street with the city hall to the left.

RECOMMENDED PRODUCERS
Domaine Schlumberger The Schlumberger wines have a high average quality. From the selection available the following wines are worth discovering: Edelzwicker Schlumberger Réserve, Sylvaner, Pinot Blanc Princes Abbés, Sylvaner, Muscat, the Rieslings Princes Abbés, Kitterlé and Saering, Tokay Pinot Gris Kitterlé, Gewurztraminers Princes Abbés, Fleur de Guebwiller, Kessler, Kitterlé, Saering. The reception hall is at 100, rue Théo-Deck.

- On a street corner near the Notre-Dame church stands the Musée du Florival (named after the valley in which Guebwiller lies). Ceramics, medieval art (such as a Madonna and Child from the 14th century), local and regional history and folklore.
- A third church of importance is the Dominican (14th century). This contains frescos and a beautiful clock tower. The church stands just to the north of the rue de la République.
- Impressive trees and many flowers can be seen in the Parc de la Marseillaise.

The terraced vineyards of the Domaine Schlumberger.

the Armagnacs abandoned after their unsuccessful attack.

Another striking church in Guebwiller is the Notre-Dame. This is actually of a far later date, namely the 18th century. A tower is missing on the outside and statues stand along the façade. The interior is worth a visit, mainly to see the extremely rich depictions of the Assumption behind the main altar.

Along Guebwiller's busy shopping street, the rue de la République, halfway between the two churches, the 16th century town hall can be found. This was built by a wealthy textile merchant in a Gothic-flamboyant style.

The north side of Guebwiller is the domain of wine: from here terraced vineyards stretch out.

RELATED TO WINE

- A small, independent producer is Hell-Cadé (14, route de Colmar, at the foot of the wine slope).
- The local wine exchange is usually organized in the first half of May.
- Of Guebwiller's three grands crus, Kitterlé enjoys the best reputation. The other two are Kessler and Saering, in that order. The wine route runs very close to Saering, which is at the junction of the roads from Bergholtz and Colmar. Here stands the 17th century Saering chapel.

RESTAURANT
Hôtel Moschenross
42 rue du Général de
Gaulle, Thann
℃ 89.37.00.86
In this large restaurant
rural dishes are mainly
served, such as snail sa-
lad with small pieces of
bacon and *meurette de
truite au Pinot Noir.*
Menus start at less than
FF 100. Also 25 hotel
rooms.

TOURIST TIPS
• From Soultz it is not
  far to Ungersheim.
  There one finds the
  Eco-musée d'Alsace, a
  marvellous open air
  museum containing
  around 50 old Alsatian
  houses.
• The Musée des Amis
  de Thann is establish-
  ed in the old Corn
  Exchange of Thann. It
  gives a most charming
  survey of local history.
• From Thann it is a 45-
  minute walk (there
  and back) to the ruins
  of the Château d'En-
  gelbourg, situated on
  a hill to the north. A
  piece of a tower lying
  on its side has recei-
  ved the nickname 'the
  eye of the witch'.

SOUTHERN HAUT-RHIN

After Guebwiller the landscape flattens out and
the vineyards disappear from view for the most
part. With the exception of one cooperative there

A small chapel in the middle of the steep Rangen vineyard.

RECOMMENDED PRODUCERS
SOULTZ
Raymond Schmitt This small winegro-
wer has some land on the grand cru Oll-
willer and makes a very successful Ries-
ling and Gewurztraminer.
WUENHEIM
Château Ollwiller The Riesling as well

as the Gewurztraminer have quality nowadays, which also holds for the Pinot
Noir.
Cooperative This firm, which operates
under the name Cave Vinicole du Vieil-Ar-
mand, has joined the *cave coopérative* of
Eguisheim. The better products include
the Riesling and Gewurztraminer Ollwil-

are almost no wine producers in the southern part of the department of Haut-Rhin: perhaps no more than ten. Touristically though, it has more to offer. Soultz was named after its salt water source. The centre, which is surrounded by the remains of ramparts, is dominated by the high, octagonal tower of the church of Saint-Maurice. This was built between the 13th and 15th centuries in Gothic style. The city hall has a double, covered outer staircase with a golden eagle (1856). Along the streets of Soultz there are many fine residences, often with bay windows. Along the wine route, near Wuenheim, lies the (closed) Château Ollwiller, rebuilt in the 18th and 20th centuries. One reaches Thann via Vieux-Thann with its smoking factories. In the heart of Thann stands Saint-Thiébaut, a collegiate church on which construction continued from the 14th century for some three centuries. Its exterior has been cleaned so that one can now fully enjoy the artistic sculpture above the main portal. The interior is rich, with splendid stained glass windows in the choir. The northern side of Thann is dominated by the extremely steep Rangen; this grand cru is the southernmost vineyard of Alsace.

The main portal of Saint-Thiébaut.

ler, as well as the Crémant.

RELATED TO WINE
• The two grands crus of southern Haut-Rhin are the Ollwiller in Wuenheim and the Rangen of Thann. The latter vineyard is considerably smaller but produces a number of exceptionally good wines. In order to taste these one must not actually be in Thann, but should visit (among others) the Domaine Zind-Humbrecht in Wintzenheim and Bernard Schoffit in Colmar, because, since the 1970s winegrowers from outside Thann have planted the once fallow Rangen.

OTHER PLACES OF INTEREST

Outside the wine area Alsace contains many places of interest. There follows a brief summary of a few of the most compelling.

MARCKOLSHEIM
- A casemate of the Maginot line functions here as both a monument and a museum.

MULHOUSE
- *Musée National de l'Automobile.* The largest collection of old cars in Europe, more than 460 examples of almost 100 different makes, including numerous Bugattis and Ferraris (192 avenue de Colmar).
- *Musée Français du Chemin de Fer.* This is the largest of its type in Europe. Next to it is a fire department museum (2 rue Alfred-de-Glehn).
- *Musée des Impressions sur Etoffes.* Enormous collection of printed fabrics from all over the world (3 rue de Bonnes-Gens).
- *Parc Zoologique et Botanique.* Splendid zoo in the middle of a park with rare trees. About one thousand animals, many of which belong to endangered species (51 rue du Jardin Zoologique).
- *Musée Historique.* Many historical articles and works of art, but also a collection of old toys. Established in the 16th century city hall (place de la Réunion).
- *Musée des Beaux-Arts.* Works by among others, Brueghel, Ruysdael and Van Dongen (4 place Guillaume-Tell).
- *Maison de la Céramique* (25 rue José-Hofer).
- *Musée de la Chapelle Saint-Jean.* Sculpture, 16th century frescos (Grand'Rue).

MURBACH
A famous and powerful monastery was established here. Only part of a Romanesque church remains, including a choir and two massive towers.

NEUF-BRISACH
Octagonal, fortified city which was built with mathematical precision
by Vauban in the 17th century. In the Porte de Belfort is a museum.

RIXHEIM
Musée du Papier Peint. Large collection of wallpaper from the 18th century, and large panoramas.

Route des Crêtes
This runs over the tops of the Vosges and
offers many distant views. It can be reached
by way of various villages and cities, such as
Kaysersberg-Orbey, Ammerschwihr-Les
Trois Epis, Turckheim-Munster, Guebwiller and Cernay-Uffoltz.

Route du Fromage
This runs through the Vosges (in part over
the Route des Crêtes) taking in no less than
30 farms which make their own Munster
cheese. These *fermes* can be recognized by a
blue sign. Most of them are also auberges
and offer visitors the opportunity to eat a
simple, nutritious lunch. The route can be
reached by following the D 10 from
Munster to the junction with the D 27 and then turning right at the
point where this comes out on the D 430.

STRASBOURG
- *Cathedral of Notre-Dame.* Its construction lasted from the 12th to the
  15th centuries. A splendid monument: a wealth of sculpture, a magnificent rose window, an astronomic clock and much more.
- *Château des Rohan.* In this 18th century building, next to the cathedral, there are three museums: Musée des Beaux-Arts (many still-
  lifes), Musée des Arts Décoratifs (striking porcelain collection),
  Musée Archéologique (prehistoric and Gallo-Romanic finds).
- *La Petite France.* A suburb full of atmosphere, with canals and half-
  timbered houses.
- *Musée Alsacien.* In this regional museum wine is accorded much pro-
  minence (23 quai Saint-Nicolas).
- *Musée Historique.* With, among other things, a three-dimensional
  city map (3 place de la Grande Boucherie).

APPENDIX

THE GRANDS CRUS

For these vineyards, which, together, account for about 10 per cent of the total area, a lower production per hectare holds. This is a maximum of 70 hectolitres, against 100 hectolitres for the rest of the area. Above all, a higher minimum alcohol percentage is prescribed (10 or 11 instead of 8.5) and only the grape varieties gewurztraminer, muscat, riesling and tokay pinot gris are allowed.

Name	*Municipality or Parish*
Altenberg de Bergbieten	Bergbieten
Altenberg de Bergheim	Bergheim
Altenberg de Wolxheim	Wolxheim
Brand	Turckheim
Bruderthal	Molsheim
Eichberg	Eguisheim
Engelberg	Dahlenheim, Scharrachbergheim
Florimont	Ingersheim, Katzenthal
Frankstein	Dambach-la-Ville
Froehn	Zellenberg
Furstentum	Kientzheim, Sigolsheim
Geisberg	Ribeauvillé
Gloeckelberg	Rodern, Saint-Hippolyte
Goldert	Gueberschwihr
Hatschbourg	Hattstatt, Voegtlinshofen
Hengst	Wintzenheim
Kanzlerberg	Bergheim
Kastelberg	Andlau
Kessler	Guebwiller
Kirchberg de Barr	Barr
Kirchberg de Ribeauvillé	Ribeauvillé
Kitterlé	Guebwiller
Mambourg	Sigolsheim
Mandelberg	Mittelwihr
Marckrain	Bennwihr, Sigolsheim
Moenchberg	Andlau, Eichhoffen
Muenchberg	Nothalten
Ollwiller	Wuenheim

Name	*Municipality or Parish*
Osterberg	Ribeauvillé
Pfersigberg	Eguisheim, Wettolsheim
Pfingstberg	Orschwihr
Praelatenberg	Kintzheim, Orschwiller
Rangen	Thann
Rosacker	Hunawihr
Saering	Guebwiller
Schlossberg	Kaysersberg, Kientzheim
Schoenenbourg	Riquewihr, Zellenberg
Sommerberg	Niedermorschwihr, Katzenthal
Sonnenglanz	Beblenheim
Spiegel	Guebwiller, Bergholtz
Sporen	Riquewihr
Steinert	Pfaffenheim, Westhalten
Steingrubler	Wettolsheim
Steinklotz	Marlenheim
Vorbourg	Rouffach, Westhalten
Wiebelsberg	Andlau
Wineck-Schlossberg	Katzenthal, Ammerschwihr
Winzenberg	Blienschwiller
Zinnkoepflé	Soultzmatt, Westhalten
Zotzenberg	Mittelbergheim

INDEX

The index consists of three parts: (1) an index of (mainly) producers and wine merchants, (2) a hotel index and (3) a restaurant index. Abbreviations: Ch. Château, Dom(s). Domaine(s).